Hal Adkins

Ain't Normal

Suzy,

Dave wanted me to personalize this book for you so I guess I will as Dave is holding a gun on me as I write. Any way Best wishes!.

Hal Adkins

P.S. send help!

Hal Adkins
Ain't Normal

By Hal Adkins

With Illustrations by Greg Wallace

Cover Photo by Kathleen Potvin
Cover art, Greg Wallace

FIRST EDITION

Published by Lulu.com

Copyright © 2011, Harold E. Adkins II

ISBN 978-257-95606-7

Acknowledgements

This book would not be possible without the help and encouragement from many people. First much thanks and appreciation goes out to the Bureau County Republican and its editor Terri Simon. She inflicted me upon the readers of the paper on a semi regular basis and as there was no or at least little mass rioting in the streets against this decision it seems to have worked out well enough but may be too early to tell. Of course being a good editor she did take out a few things from certain stories that would not be befitting of a family type newspaper. I have of course put them all back, plus a few more.

Donna Celaya, who is a hell of a good writer and judge of talent, receives much kudos for encouraging me to get started in this form of literary expression in the first place. She has always enjoyed and praised my work although I trust her judgment on writing matters she also believes that I am a really good looking fellow so apparently her perception is not always 100%.

The girlfriend Kathy Potvin for many years now has put up with my ranting, raving and great waving about of arms in the air, with much patience and quiet dignity although I'm sure the thought balloons above her head tell an entirely different story. Thanks so much for not pushing me off the boat to Key West when you had the chance.

Also to all the fans and various people who have said for years I should write a book, well here it is now quit your whining.

And then there's Greg Wallace who has more artistic talent in his pinky finger than anyone I personally know. We seem to have a similar sense of humor which is either a gateway to tremendously entertaining works of art and literature from us both, or possible felony charges.

Foreword

Many of these works of semi-literary art (?) have appeared as columns on the pages and online at the *Bureau County Republican*, Princeton, IL whose editor Terri Simon and publisher Sam Fisher surely must have been desperate for something, anything to fill out their pages, at least that's the rumor. Several of these stories/experiences have taken place in and around my home town of La Moille, Illinois (population 800) and at or on the way to and from various road racing courses where I have competed in wheel to wheel racing events in a formula car. And the rest I just make up because I can.

After having been a professional photographer for over 30 years I decided to expand my creative horizons while I still have, hopefully, ample brain cells to do so although some would argue it is already too late. This book is intended to entertain, and dare I say...yes, yes I will, enlighten in a hopefully humorous way the clamoring human masses who may be seeking a warm and comforting diversion from the day-to-day travails of life. A work of words to perhaps bring back remembrance's of one's own past times and personal human history experiences. And maybe, just maybe help create a dialogue between the generations that so often are sadly divided along troubled generational lines in this modern world we live in. Also to maybe help family and friends become once again closer to each other, to put aside past differences and just enjoy a few good stories. This is my hope, my prayer for the readers of this book.

Okay, mostly I would like to be able to make enough bucks from this writing thing to be able to get the hell out of Illinois in the winter and spend quality time in Florida playing volleyball in the sand and mixing up a fresh batch of Mojitos for "Happy Hour" at the trailer park.

About the artist.

Greg Wallace was born near the small hamlet of Walnut, Illinois. Being the youngest of three boys and a girl, the child became a constant target of never-ending wedgies and noogies. Revenge for this continuous torture was the main reason our young hero started putting crayon to paper. Armed with his box of Crayolas, he would soon learn how to draw his brothers with big noses and his evil hag of a sister with a truly monstrous butt.

Throughout his formative years, the growing boy found he could bring smiles to people's faces with his cartoons and caricatures. He would fill his mother's kitchen table with papers full of doodles of friends and teachers. Upon finding one of the lad's more creative offerings, a rather exasperated geography teacher (with a big nose) asked, "Do you plan on doing this for a living Mr. Wallace?" The aspiring artist looked him right in his massive proboscis and answered with a resounding, "uh-huh."

From being a caricature artist at Six Flags Great America in Gurnee, Illinois to his present position as Graphic Design Editor for the Bureau County Republican in Princeton, Illinois and all of his years of creating freelance artwork from his home-based studio in Walnut, Illinois, Greg has followed his passion for creating art. He has won numerous awards from the Illinois Press Association, Northern Illinois Newspaper Association and the Suburban Newspaper Association in the categories of editorial cartooning, illustration and graphic design.

Greg resides in his childhood hometown of Walnut, Illinois with his wife Joyce, son Zack, daughter Izzy and a stupid cat.

Testimonials

Michael Moore: Don't bother reading anything this capitalist idiot writes, obviously he has his head stuck up his...oh, yes I will have some more fried chicken please. Hey buddy, you gonna finish that pork chop?

Speaker of the House, John Boehner: This book makes me cry, but then again what doesn't.

Rosie O'Donnell: Hey, I had dibs on that pork chop.

Al Gore: Hal does not have a clue to what is really happening to the world's climate, not a clue, He is naïve and not acting in a responsible fashion by making light of global warming and other rinky-dink issues of major importance and income to me and the other residents here in LaLa Land...yeah I know it's July and it's 54 degrees outside, what's your point?

Usama Bin Laden: What do I care about this book, I'm dead.

Former Speaker of the House Nancy Pelosi: Am I wide eyed and excited looking because I read Hal's book? Oh heavens no, I haven't read it yet, truth is I never read anything and always have the facial expression of someone who has just had a ferret stuffed down their underwear.

Trace Adkins: Yeah we're probably related, ain't proud of it but seems like I got all the good looks and talent.

Michael Moore: No, seriously man, you gonna finish that?

Former President George W. Bush: Uh...yeah...this guy, could be, the next, ah, Dave Bernie.

Dave Barry: That's Barry you knucklehead. Hal is not fit to, and I am not making this up, lick my sneakers, which would be a great name for a rock and roll band.

Usama Bin Laden: ...hello...I'm still dead...

Chumlee, from *Pawn Stars:* In essence I believe Mr. Adkins has captured an intriguing cornucopia of life through his own experiences and oft times caustic opinions. He has written them down with a vibrant vitriol that can at once be most thought-provoking, adroit, deliciously succinct and always immensely entertaining. And keep your @&#*ing damn hands off my pork chop, Moore.

Sarah Palin: I can see Hal from my house...kidding! No wait, he's stumbling around in my front yard...what the hell?

Larry the Cable Guy: Now listen here, I have read some pretty he-larious stuff before, things that make tears run down my cheeks and near peed my pants. Well this ain't one of 'em but maybe someday Hal will git er done!

Michael Moore: Who's up for tacos?

Rosie O'Donnell: I'll drive.

Contents

If we couldn't laugh we would all go insane.

Changes in latitudes changes in attitudes.

Jimmy Buffett: 1977

The History Channell, expanding your mind and your pants.

HAL ADKINS; CIRCA 1975

The other night I watched a show on the History Channel about George Washington Carver, I first learned about this gentleman in grade school. George Washington Carver did a lot of clever things with peanuts. He developed hundreds of uses for products made from the simple peanut, including the first commercially available fully edible ear plugs.

I love peanuts and as I watched the show I was completely overwhelmed with just one thought. Why the hell did I vote for Jimmy Carter, twice? No, actually I had a huge desire to have some peanuts. All I had in the house was peanut butter, the good natural healthy kind made with no preservatives and has to be mixed by hand in the jar then refrigerated. I am no G.W. Carver but it is my firm belief this natural health food can be made even healthier by the addition of a bit of honey and some extra salt.

So there I sat at 9:30 in the evening eating cold peanut butter with a spoon out of a jar. I was simply compelled by the subject matter, which reminded me of other compulsions related to the History Channel.

First there was the show on the soft drink industry. I instantly developed a powerful urge to have a Coke. I don't consume a lot of soft drinks, but my tongue was crying out for the stuff. I seldom keep any around as I try to consume healthier fare, such as extra salty honey flavored peanut butter. I did check but had none of the fizzy enamel killer on hand.

I soon got over this urge however as the next show immediately following the soft drink expose was an hour on the history of brewing beer. Now we're talking a more age appropriate beverage. The thought of sipping on a cold frosty thirst quenching glass of refreshing liquid made from fermented plants sounded like a real winner. I had a moderate supply of low carb brew in the refrigerator which sounded way better than a soda anyway.

I think of low carb beer as health food, but none-alcoholic beer to me is just something tasting kind of like beer, and I have no interest in it personally because it sounds about as appealing as trying to make southern fried chicken out of tofu.

With the availability of the shows subject matter I was able to successfully participate hands, or mouth on in the history of beer lesson, which caused me to fall asleep in the recliner although I did rouse myself long enough to catch part of the next show which involved the distilling of hard liquor, but luckily conked out again before I could do myself any serious harm. After that was an episode on ice cream and of course I had none of this on hand either because I am *Mr. Healthy Guy.*

Trying to eat healthy is such a challenge. I remember starting to watch an interesting History Channel program on how the frozen vegetables industry was developed, and that particular episode did in fact inspire me to change my life and eating habits. No wait, I changed the channel, figured it was easier.

Another show along these lines I really enjoyed perhaps too much was the history of snack foods. I learned a lot about potato chips, pretzels, snack crackers, potato chips, cookies, and of course potato chips. This time I got up and drove to the store to get a big bag of those thinly sliced salty tator snacks. Now, I can make a meal out of those things if I let myself, and did. Washed it down with a biggie soft drink I picked up as long as I was at the store anyway. Also got a big can of peanuts, small bottle of liquor, half gallon of ice cream, another six pack of beer, box of cookies and some genuine tofu free southern fried chicken.

By the time I got home and spread out my high caloric History Channel homework on the various flat surfaces of my weight lifting machine and treadmill, but within easy reach from recliner, I was set for pleasant afternoon into evening of History Channel viewing pleasure. And what was the first show that came on but a disturbing and lurid history of drug cultures from around the world.

I have to tell you I changed the channel immediately as that sort of lifestyle is not something I have any interest in at all. To me getting high is not smart, fun, or funny. It is detrimental to ones physical and mental well being and no way to go through life. Anyone extolling any kind of excessive consumptive life style obviously has some sort of substance abuse problem and needs professional help!

I was quite content to just sit and watch an old Cheech and Chong movie surrounded by my good friends the Millers, Mr. Daniels, the Lay's family, those nutty Haagen Dazs guys, Keebler elves, the Colonel and of course 'Ol peanut head, Jimmy Carter.

Keeping it healthy, that's what I do. Pass the Pepto please...

Yes, actually I am that kind of guy

WARNING: May cause headaches, death, or worse!

We are seeing more and more advertisement for various medications and most all of them seem to spend half of the commercial telling us, well scaring us really about the possible side effects, and many of these side effects appear to be at least as bad or worse than your medical malady. For example, you start out with a couple of zits on your forehead, apply some of _Dr. Craterface's Purple Pimple Plaster,_ something goes horribly wrong and before long you end up looking like your mom has been feeding you frozen peas with a slingshot.

Some of the medical problems you may be trying to alleviate are serious enough that the risk is worth taking, but you must be educated! Warnings of these risks and consequences of side effects are normally included in an extremely detailed notice sheet of some sort within the product packaging and are often times as big as a Texas road map, or roughly half the size of Michael Moore's shorts.

Imagine a headache has you hurting bad, so you decide to try the new headache and pain reliever advertised on TV, *Improved Double Strength Pain Pulverize, Kill or Cure Formula.* Sounds like it might help ease the pain in the brain, but better read the possible side affects first. WARNING: *Use of this product may cause skin irritations, nausea, headaches... blindness, hearing loss, and hallucinations involving a giant disembodied pulsing brain chasing you down the street in your underwear. If you cannot tolerate aspirin you should not be consuming this product as it is nothing more than a big honk'n chunk of aspirin the size of a walnut, and may eat a hole in your guts. If this were to happen please consider using our stomach medication, New, Super Hole in Your Guts Patch, whose active ingredients include fiberglass, vinyl, and radiator stop leak. Consult your mechanic before use.*

Having trouble sleeping at night? Take the newly formulated, *Sleep Like the Living Dead, Part II.*

CAUTION: *This medication may cause drowsiness, (ya think?) anxiety, stomach cramps, headaches, and sleeplessness... Other possible side effects may include short and long term memory loss (something to remember), a complete, irreversible, total and permanent shut down of the circulatory and respiratory systems along with the total cessation of all brain functions resulting in your body assuming room temperature. May also cause death.*

Feeling a little out of sorts in your ability to cope with life around you? You and your multiple personalities having a difficult time getting along? Simple, just buy some *Jung and Freud Super Psychotic Chill Pills!* Guaranteed to make your own little world work in complete harmony with the universe around you, and you, and you...

NOTICE: *This product may cause cramps, headaches, and psychotic reactions, like that creepy crawly feeling as if there were a bunch of disgusting and weird little worms swarming all over your worthless body, but they're not there at all, really, it is just your imagination. Trust us. May also cause euphoria and the temporary feeling that you could go out and conquer the world, but you know that's not true and is never going to happen because you can't even run your own miserable day to day existence without taking a pill, you insignificant little worm. Speaking of that, there really IS a bunch of disgusting and weird little worms swarming all over your worthless body right now because we put them there when you were stoned on <u>Sleep Like The Living Dead, Part II</u>. Ha! Couldn't happen to a more deserving species of sub-human bottom feeding slime than you! And that was no hallucination; a giant disembodied pulsing brain wearing your underwear actually WAS chasing you down the street last night! May also cause excessive misreading and misinterpretation of warning labels. Long term use of this product may result in a feeling of inferiority, so be careful...loser.*

Hair a little thin on the top? No problem, Just apply some <u>*German Formula Just for Skinheads Hair Growth Treatment,*</u> and your comb will be smoke'n in no time.

WARNING: *This product has not been approved or found to provide verifiable results by the FDA, AMA, FHA, NEA, CIA, NBA, IRA, AA, or any other organization ending in A, although it has been shown to be 100% more successful than Michael Moore's weight loss program. In fact is has only been tested on animals, cats specifically. Shaved cats. Did you ever try and shave a cat? Ha, good luck! Anyway, we shaved a few cats and then applied this stuff and they grew some hair. Okay, technically it was fur, but it grew so we put the product on the market. Probably work as well as anything else out there you think will grow your stupid hair back. But be careful, application of this product may cause you to hiss at the dog, stay up all night fighting in the backyard, mainline catnip, knock over trash cans, and lick your private parts in front of guests. If any of the above happens in excess we suggest you be neutered. If you don't have any hair you're not going to get a date anyway...loser.*

If it was not for women men would be a lot more scared of death.

Saving you from a Valentine's Day massacre...maybe.

Valentine's Day is just around the empty chocolate wrapper and lace undies strewn corner. Judging by the divorce rate and orders of protection issued nationwide last year, I believe more than a few of you people could use some help. Let's *Ask Hal.*

Dear Hal: Last year I gave my wife some chocolate for Valentine's Day. A lot of chocolate. In fact it came in a bucket that said Extra Large Tub O'Chocolate. Along with that I gave her a nice card that said she was the biggest thing that ever happened to me and there was a huge place in my heart reserved just for her. She was very upset and angry with me for some reason and that has not gone away. What did I do wrong, and how can I get some excitement back in our marriage? Signed, <u>Clueless and Confused.</u>

Dear CC: Let's review. Okay first thing I see is the words extra large, tub, biggest, and huge. What are you, some kind of moron? Any use of these words at anytime throughout the year much less on Valentine's Day may cause you to find your dumb you know what sleeping on the couch and living on a steady diet of stale Cheetos. Women are sensitive to this type of thing, and whenever you are asked the dreaded question, "does this dress make my you know what look like and extra large tub," it is in your best interest to fake a heart attack, or actually have one as it is less painful and life threatening than giving her an answer…any answer. So this year buy her one small low calorie protein bar with a nice hand written personalized card attached to it that says, *Dear, (Her name here)* I love you this much, and also want you to know you will always be twice the size 9 woman I married!" Presto, there will be excitement! Trust me.

Dear Hal: My husband is a sports fanatic. I can't get him to pay much attention to me on Valentine's Day or any other day for that matter as he is usually watching some game on TV in the evening and on weekends too. I am starving for some physical attention and secretly getting very desperate. I was thinking maybe a little strip tease in front of the TV would produce some results. Think that would work? Signed, <u>Unloved and Unnoticed.</u>

Dear Unloved and Unnoticed: Absolutely. That will work like a charm and get you lots of attention, but only over at the neighbor's house, especially if his wife is home. A crowded sports bar would likely work even better, and don't worry; your secret life of desperation is safe with me.

Dear Hal: My wife says she wants to go out this year for Valentine's Day. I was thinking a quick burger at Carl's

Cardiac Shack then on to the monster truck show. Maybe after that a couple of beers at the local strip joint would be nice. What do you think? Signed, Mister Romantic.

Dear Mister R: Works for me. Run that itinerary by the wife and if she doesn't go for it pick me up about 7:00, but I suggest we go to the sports bar. I think Unloved and Unnoticed is going to be there and she's desperate.

Dear Hal: Last year I asked you for advice on what to give my wife for Valentine's Day. You suggested giving her a hand written personalized card and gave me an example of what to write. She appeared to be quite angry when reading the first part of the card where I wrote, Dear, her name here. She called me a moron. I wrote it just how you told me, but she was obviously very upset with me. So, genius, what are your brilliant thoughts on the matter this year? Please don't make me look like a moron again. Signed, Tom Cruise.

Dear Tom: That mission's impossible. You are a moron.

Dear Hal: My boyfriend is a NASCAR fanatic. What would you suggest as an appropriate stock car racing related gift to give him for Valentine's Day? Signed, Daytona Donna.

Dear Double D: A full set of teeth. No, just kidding. A nice new razor so he can have his favorite driver's car number shaved into the hair on his back would be a great gift. Just kidding…. No, actually I'm not.

Remember, in the book of *What Men Know About Women,* all pages are blank.

Dating tips: Stop and smell the weeds.

We have all done this at some point in our lives and many of us still avail ourselves of this oft time's fun activity as it can be both exciting and scary all at the same time. I am of course talking about driving through town naked. No, not really but now I have your attention, and the above is not nearly as scary and exciting as the real subject matter; dating.

I have been dating off and on since the last century when I had more hair, a red Camaro, and a wonderful, blissful ignorance of women's needs – much like present day - so I feel I have some knowledge and experience on the subject at least from a guy's standpoint. Perhaps this knowledge will help other men in successfully navigating the dating waters while clearing up some of the misconceptions women have, real or imagined, that we men have the intelligence and compassion of dead weeds.

Getting the Date: Gentlemen, let's first assume that every woman you meet is *not* just dying to go out with you. Some rejection may be suffered on the first initial query to if the lovely lady you have your eye on would indeed like to spend some hopefully, quality time with you. Here's a quick tutorial on if you have a chance to "make a date."

If your lady of interest after the first suggestion by you to "get together sometime," says "maybe," "we'll see," or, "that could be fun," you might be in. If on the other hand the response is, "sorry, I don't date out of my species, monkey boy," "not even if I was in a coma," or "do you smell dead weeds?" you *may* have struck out, and hysterical laughter indicates she is likely not enthralled with your faded paisley tank top and comb over. If she punches in 3 numbers on her cell phone while muttering something about "order of protection," there is the remote possibility she might not be interested or at the very least playing extremely hard to get so don't give up hope, but do hasten quickly from the immediate area, monkey boy.

We will assume you have actually been able to arrange a date and a mutually agreed upon time for the adventure to begin. Caution: Try and get to the arranged meeting place to pick her up as close to the scheduled time as possible. A few minutes early is best, a few minutes late is okay, but if late by half an hour or more you better show up with your head wrapped in bandages or be missing a limb, and be able to produce a Doctors written explanation for being tardy along with X-rays and lab test results.

Not being ready and on time for a date is just not a cool thing, guys. Of course it is totally acceptable and indeed standard operating procedure for women.

A word on the etiquette of opening and closing car doors; when on a date it is very important to always do this promptly and with style, gentlemen. Bonus points may be awarded if besides your own you open and close hers too. However for people over 50 who drive low slung sporty type cars, it is common courtesy that whoever manages to crawl out first should help to extricate the other.

Talking Points. While dating and especially on a first date independent studies have shown the best thing for men to do in regards to conversations with women is to just shut up. Whatever you say is on average wrong approximately 87-92 % of the time, it can and will be held against you. These studies were conducted primarily by women who are still ticked off about not being asked to the prom in 1967.

Examples: While commenting on how nice she looks, do not refer to her hair-do with comments containing the phrases "eraser head," or "poodle hair," no matter how obvious the resemblance.

When discussing your favorite movies or TV shows, try not to use the words, "chick-flick crap," as your date may be an intelligent, sensitive and caring individual, who might actually enjoy watching chick-flick crap.

Avoid mentioning old girlfriends but if you must just say, "it didn't work out." The words "court appearance," "visitations rights," and "contagious" will shut down the conversation faster than it takes to get a penicillin shot.

On where to go: Standard destinations for a date might involve a restaurant for dinner and perhaps an optional movie before or after the meal. Show some manners fellas, when at the fine dining establishment of your choice carry her tray to the booth AND fill her cup at the soda dispenser. DO NOT at any time mention the words, "super size."

Choices for movies can be tricky. A comedy is a good bet, but if in a weak moment you let her drag your reluctant ass to a chick flick, slouch down in the theater seat a bit so your head won't snap back when sleepy time comes, and upon waking if you want to show your sensitive side or pretend to have one, after you notice a sniffle and a tear coming from your date, a quick yank on a nose hair (yours...) will yield the same results on your part without having to fake any emotional involvement.

At the end of the evening, when in doubt, a good hug will do in lieu of a kiss. But if after the fourth or fifth date you are still getting nothing but hugs, you just have to be honest and say to your date, "Look, Sister Mary Roberta, it's just not working out, sorry...but you do look stunning in black and white."

Chalk it up to experience, feel a little tinge of sadness as you leave the Convent, then drive your Camaro naked through town, smelling the real or imagined yet pungent fragrance of dead weeds along the way.

I fear that as I grow older I am turning into a dirty old man, but as I was a dirty young man the transition has been going relatively smoothly.

More dating tips, giving compliments...what's that smell?

In this installment on dating we are going to explore the right and wrong things for you, a guy, to say to your lady in the opening stages of a budding relationship, specifically the first few dates after the initial mistake she made in agreeing to go out with you in the first place.

Although a lot of this could be helpful to men in an advanced and terminally long relationship such as marriage, the following tips on making compliments are more for the guy who doesn't know compliments from compost, although both will smell mightily if not handled and applied properly.

Men involved in long lasting relationships of any kind, especially marriage have by now probably said about all of the stupid things in their life they are going to say starting with, "I do." To their women handlers men are hopelessly brain dead subservient idiots, this according to a recent survey conducted by an organization called *Women to Improve Men's Perpetual Shortcomings,* or *W.I.M.P.S.* Their motto; "We have to tear you down to build you up... Nah, we're kidding, we really just like tearing you down."

Regarding your date's general appearance upon picking her up, what WILL WORK: *"You look nice."* This is very non-committal and non-confrontational which is extremely important. Try to use the word "nice" instead of "swell" or it could be interpreted as mocking and disingenuous. What WON'T WORK: *"Wow, you look hot!"*

Now keep in mind she has spent at a minimum six hours bathing, doing her hair, applying make-up with a putty knife, spray painting her nails and viewing herself in the mirror 147 times while trying to decide just the perfect outfit to wear. All of this in an effort to look, well, hot.

You of course are not allowed to notice or make mention of this as she will immediately accuse you of being a sexist pig or worse, related to Charlie Sheen and tell you in great detail how and why you have to change your attitude! And she will tell you this until blood is running out of your ears and you pray for death.

On her choice of perfume, this is what WILL WORK: *"The perfume you are wearing is terrific, what's it called?"* What WON'T WORK: *"What's that smell?"* This is especially egregious if there is no perfume involved.

On her wardrobe, SAY THIS: *"That material and color really complements your beautiful complexion."* NOT THIS: *"I didn't know The Salvation Army store carried maternity dresses."*

If you both become a little giddy after a couple of drinks with your meal and you want to be romantic, SAY THIS: *"As the evening goes on you just seem to have this alluring glow about you that I can't help but notice."* NOT THIS: *"Wow, are you getting really liquored up or what!"* Unless she *is* getting really liquored up or what, then she won't notice or care. And if she seems to have forgotten your name this would be a good time to ask if you could borrow a few bucks, then graciously offer to pay the tab, with her money.

Along the lines of general conversation, TRY THIS: *"You are so easy to talk to. I feel we could sit here all night looking into each other eyes and sharing our life stories and dreams for the future."* NOT THIS: *"You know, the more I drink the better you look."* Even if you are sincere.

It's acceptable to politely inquire about her background, family, friends, her work, etc., but SAY THIS: *"So, have you lived around here your whole life? Where did you go to school? I just want to get to know all about you."*

NOT THIS: *"So, you haven't dated in awhile, must have something to do with that cold sore thing, huh?*

In summation: Be sure your complimentary words make her feel like she is the most important person in the room, no, the world! Let her know you are focused on nothing but her and her alone, and she is what makes your little heart go pitter-patter. That's right gentlemen, LIE!

Even if she looks like she just crawled out of some back street cardboard refrigerator box after a 48 hour date with *Jack Daniels* and her perfume reminds you of *Dollar Store* mosquito repellent. Even if her makeup appears to have been applied with a broom by *Vampyra Queen of the Dead* and you recognize her dress as the one your mom gave to *The Salvation Army* seven years ago. Even if her hair looks like it has been styled with a *Dust Buster,* LIE!

Most men know a good and well executed relationship lie is a great tool to massage your ladies ego, smooth tensions, and can often be very useful in responding with great compassion and feeling to many important, serious, yet incredibly stupid and meaningless conversations.

Now you might feel a little guilty about being less than honest with her compliments because she has always been so genuinely complimentary to you, remember?

Like when you picked her up for your date last weekend and she said you looked really buff in your *XXL* relaxed fit *Thunder Butt* jeans. She also thinks bald guys like you with a comb over and mutton chop sideburns are very hot, and the cologne you bought at the truck stop was really swell.

Bless her heart. You know she's a wonderful woman and just might be a keeper as she has always been very forthcoming with her compliments about you, right?

What's that smell?

Warmth is life. Cold is where you store dead stuff.

Running barefoot through the wind chill.

YOU'LL SNOWMOBILE YOUR EYE OUT KID

The chill wind blows the golden leaves, not so long before were the color of green and summer gone, across the now barren yards and into the gray and colorless streets. Where luxuriant grass once yielded the intoxicating emerald essence of freshly mown blades, there is now darkened yet to tan and brown, a sea of dormant lawns where once children running barefoot across the lush summer grass giggled with innocent joy and delight. Sidewalks, once teeming with happy people enjoying a summer's eve stroll while drinking in the warm golden sunset and in turn become enveloped by the black satin warmth when darkness crossed the landscape as in the final closing act curtain of a serene nocturnal play, are empty now.

And why.

And why.

Because it's damn freaking cold, that's why.

Seems as I become more and more calendarically challenged, winter becomes increasingly abusive to my psyche. I swear as November nears its end and it gets colder all there seems to be out there on the landscape are varying and depressing shades of tan, black, white and gray, and this leads to more swearing.

Wasn't always this way. Back in the last century...ewww, hurts to hear myself say that, when I was a kid cold weather simply meant you played differently. We put away the bikes, roller skates, fishing poles and BB guns, ok we never put those away as there was always something that needed shooting, and got out the sleds and ice skates.

Ah, that first exhilarating speedy sled ride down a really long hill, which often was maybe one of two runs because it was way too much trouble to trudge back up and do it again. We would normally then just start a camp fire and shoot something. Then there was the challenge to see who could ice skate down a frozen creek the farthest without falling down or breaking through the ice, followed by fire and shooting.

With skates laced up nice and tight so our ankles would not wobble back and forth and get sore, off we would go on a frosty afternoon. But no matter how tight we laced them up you could always tell the next day at school the kids who had been creek running on the ice by their painful steps, smoky essence, and oft times BB gun welts.

Add in snowball fights contested within the confines of snow forts and tunnels along with gorgeous scenery and winter was not such a bad thing when you were young, innocent...and dumb.

Then you get older and have to get to work and your car won't start, or you slide in the ditch or you can't see out of the quarter inch of ice covering the windshield and the defroster is barely working and the vinyl seats are hard and cold, yada, yada. Add in drifted over driveways and lanes, some frozen pipes, power outages, high heating bills and the occasional incidents of falling on your ass trying to make your way down an icy sidewalk and you find yourself wondering how you *ever* thought winter was fun.

So like me a lot of people in the wintertime find themselves staying inside as much as possible and generally hibernating on the couch during the cold months watching TV and dreaming of summers glorious return, while attempting to grasp the concept of how there could be a difference of temps outside from say July and August and the stone cold dead of winter, of well over 100 degrees.

I used to lie on the couch and listen to the snowmobilers go by and say to myself, "Crazy bastards!" But being a mechanical type of guy and possibly suffering a blow to the head that I cannot to this day remember happening, I got interested in...snowmobiles.

I've always enjoyed a good project so found a not so good running older sled in October for $150, fixed what was wrong with it, ordered a few new parts, slapped on some fresh paint, drove around the dormant lawn where once I ran barefoot across the lush summer grass giggling with innocent joy and delight, and forgive me Oh Mighty Lord of the Heat Index, prayed for snow.

Damned if it didn't snow quite considerably that November and stayed so the snowmobiling season was on and I was inexplicably delighted. Took a few chilly short rides with other "sledders" and mastered the exciting and challenging art of local snowmobiling, commonly and colorfully called, "Ohnoimtipingover" which is also Midwest Speak for, *crap, this is gonna really hurt,* and after having my right leg nearly ripped off by a passing corn stalk, the machine was sold before Christmas for $400 and I was back on the couch saying to myself, "Crazy bastards, but now I have enough money for a really good BB gun! Who wants to start a fire?"

You know a couple of words never used in conjunction in the warmer months are wind and chill. Wind is in basic reference to most any kind of breeze including the ones generated while spending quality time up on two wheels on a warm day of motorcycling. Chill is a great thing to do to any beverage you choose to enjoy after the above mentioned ride.

Now in the winter *wind* and *chill* fit together very well to describe the lethal combination of recorded outside temp and velocity of the wind to produce the equivalent feeling of that wind-chill factor temperature on the bare skin of anyone brain dead enough to still be wearing shorts in the winter. A motorcycle induced cool breeze is one thing, speeding along on a snowmobile *making my own wind-chill* is quite another, but at least I had my pants on most of the time. So be careful and have fun out there all you winter sports crazies, but I'm staying on the couch and pre-giggling over next summer.

It doesn't happen often but whenever I feel a bit of an urge get back on one of those tracked refrigeration units I just stick my head out the window of my car while driving down some snow strewn highway until I can't feel my nose, and my brain(?) freeze gets me to having visions of a future life in a warmer winter climate with a license plate encompassing the words "snow" and "bird." Then I'm over it.

Tee-hee...

Apparently 70 is the new 50. 60 is when you start telling everyone that 70 is the new 50.

A really tall stump.

GERONIMO!

Normally I am not a seeker of thrills, as in that adrenalin junky stuff, although sometimes exciting moments just happen, like when I was crawling under an electric fence and accidentally touched it with my head, made quite a loud humming sound actually. That was exciting along with really annoying and may have altered my reasoning power as another exciting thing I did was jump out of an airplane. On purpose. Once.

My youthful pursuance of cheap thrills pretty much ended at the age of thirteen after an unfortunate incident at fair involving a corn dog, big orange drink, a Tilt-A-Whirl, and the back of the nearest tent. But many years later the offer was made to take a day long course in skydiving and make a jump at the end of the day. It would be just a short airplane ride then leap into the atmosphere with nothing to stop my fall but several large pieces of man-made synthetic material, and many feet of cord about as big around as a pencil lead, all manufactured by people of unknown origin, and packed together by some stranger who thinks falling from the sky at 120 mph is fun. What could possibly go wrong?

The school was provided free of charge to me and I was going to do a magazine article about the experience and get paid. Of course the word *paid* always trumps the words *reason* and *common sense.* Ask anyone in government.

Had to drive in a very thick morning fog to the airport hangar where the school was to be held and you can't fly planes and jump out of them in a fog. Unfortunately the weather did not cooperate for the entire rest of the day. It cleared up.

First on the agenda was to watch a movie on skydiving with a dozen or so classmates who apparently were also at one time or another victims of some type of electrical mishap such as mine, and then more comments were made and questions answered by our main instructor and jumpmaster who incidentally was walking with a limp as he had slightly injured himself while, strange as it sounds, skydiving. I could feel the excitement welling up inside of me, or it might have just been breakfast.

We practiced exiting the airplane we were going to be using, and then we jumped off of a stump for awhile to practice how to land. We were also told by a gentleman with a peculiarly high voice to make sure the crotch strap on the chute harness was cinched up very snug so as not to cause, um, discomfort and injury upon the chute snapping open.

Although the course was just a day long it really was quite complete and by the end of the day I actually thought that perhaps this might make a nice new pastime to indulge in as all the farmers in my rural neighborhood no longer had any electric fences to provide me with a suitable head hum.

We all assembled at the jump site and my group of three jumpers was third in line to go. We watched from the ground as the first couple trips aloft went relatively well. One fellow had his chute not open quite all the way on one side so he came down while spinning in circles like a Tilt-A-Whirl, but he hadn't dined on corn dog and big orange drink for lunch so he was fine and just as well as there was no tent nearby.

Once aloft the nervousness took over then reached a crescendo pitch shortly after the guy right ahead of me exited the plane and the realizations set in that I was well and truly next and *had* to do it.

Now, I am a pretty daring fellow, sometimes, but I had the sensation of feathers growing all over my body and the feeling like I might just lay a giant egg, or it could have just been lunch, but right there in the open doorway were vivid scenes of my life flashing by against a background of pretty blue sky and white fluffy clouds. But I am more chicken of being chicken than stepping away from a perfectly good flying airplane. I apparently also have less functioning brain cells than the average squash...maybe squash is not a good word to use when referencing skydiving.

The jumpmaster asked if I was ready to go. "Cluck!" Was about the only sound I could muster.

After working my way out on the strut of the airplane and hanging there for a moment (I hear deep imprints of my fingers are in that strut to this very day) with my feet blowing in the wind and nothing but vast corn fields 3000 feet below me, I let go. Well technically I couldn't hold on any longer.

As this was a static line jump the ripcord was attached by a strap to the plane so I fell just a short ways before the chute automatically began to open. After the chute opened fully and I started breathing again I found I had not wet myself, much, and had no discernable crotch strap discomfort. It was actually quite pleasant to be drifting quietly in the sky taking in the view.

We were supposed to follow signals from the ground to help us steer the chute to the target landing area, but being a licensed pilot I just flew it my way, what do they know. We were told to pull the steering cords to "flair" the chute just before landing to make contacting the ground a bit softer when we were eight to ten feet off the ground. Well that was easy, I just pulled about the time my feet hit the top of the tall corn, and only a scant quarter of a mile away from the target too. Nobody else missed it by that much the entire day. They said it was a new state record and third overall nationally.

I know, I know. A lot of people do this and have a great time. They say the free fall from much higher altitudes is the best part and is just like flying. To me it is similar to falling off a 3000 foot stump.

Sometimes the thought occurs to me that maybe I should try it again to at least make up for my somewhat displaced landing, but instead I just stick my tongue in a light socket and when I wake up I can't remember why I ever thought jumping out of a perfectly good flying airplane was a good idea in the first place.

Note to anyone in government thinking of trying skydiving, remember: Six to eight inches of slack in the crotch strap is just about right, yeah.

I had a teacher who once said to me, "Hal, always stay humble. In your case it will probably come in handy."

I hear that whistle blow'n or; how the cat and I got lucky.

We didn't start out looking for quite this much adventure, but as teenage guys we were wild carefree hooligans wanting to raise a handful of heck on a hot summer Saturday afternoon.

We were nuts, berserk even. We jolly well wanted to rampage and did not care what people thought of us, which worked out okay because nobody thought much about us anyhow, but if they did I'm sure they figured we were berserk hooligans. We decided to go for broke, throw caution to the wind! We rode our bikes out to the woods to walk around.

To walk around in these particular woods a creek had to be crossed and there were three ways this could be accomplished. We could wade through the creek, walk over the top of a railroad trestle that crossed the creek, or walk the planks that went through the trestle. Adventure has its limits of discomfort so getting wet didn't get any votes.

Going over the top was always a good option but was a scary forty feet high and we would have been in deep...peril if a big honk'n train were to try and occupy the same space on the trestle at the same time the *Berserk Boys With No Brains* were rampaging across it crying for their mommas.

But of course being in our middle teens we thought of ourselves as immortal, and were destined to lead perfect and idyllic lives, nothing bad or scary was ever going to happen to us. This was of course in the times before marriage, children, and the 2008 elections.

As there was no rush to get to the woods, we started a slow ramble across the planks just below the ties and rails, chatting about things I can't tell you about here as (1) I don't remember, and (2) I'm sure they were disgusting and crude teenage boy stuff involving hooliganism and rampaging. Whatever we were talking about came to an abrupt halt when in the distance we heard an unmistakable sound, the low moan of a TRAIN HORN!

Under normal circumstances, normal defined here as not on the verge of being run over by a train, that howling horn was a clarion call to quickly find something to lay on the tracks and see how big and flat it could get.

Pennies were a favorite choice, as they would get as big as a quarter, and quarters as big as silver dollars, and I'm sure the neighbor's cat we borrowed would have gotten as big as a mountain lion if we could have persuaded it to sit on the track a little longer, and the duct tape would have held. Anyway on that occasion the train horn scared it off and it headed briskly towards the woods with a vengeful gleam in its really big eyes.

As the three of us scrambled quickly to reach the other end of the trestle I knew how that cat felt, except for the part about the duct tape. I bet we were all thinking the same thing too...just what the heck is a hooligan anyway?

No, actually it was that we were damn lucky we did not choose to go over the top as we would have had only three options to keep us from becoming scary looking hood ornaments on the westbound Burlington Northern freight.

The first two choices being to jump about 40 feet into the creek, or run like hell. The flaws in both these choices were the waste deep water would not have slowed our decent very well, but as we would have been wet all over anyway any terror driven "mishaps" would have been nicely blended and therefore camouflaged thus keeping our adolescent cat snatching dignity intact.

Running on railroad ties that have nothing but a lot of air between them is tricky at best as every step would have to be dead on the ties, or we would be dead on the rails!

The third option of course would have been to wait for the train to swerve.

So having a train that weighed about 3 gazillion tons traveling at an estimated 900 mph passing about 14 inches over our stupid yet wildly exaggerating the situation teenage heads was oddly, a good thing. But we also thought stuffing lit fire crackers down each other's shorts, and duct taping Bootsy to a railroad track were good things too.

We reached the last plank but had no time to climb down, and as the train's arrival was imminent we just sat and waited. About then it got increasingly noisy and there was a lot of violent shaking going on, although I don't think the other guys even noticed I was doing it.

You think a train is noisy as it goes by you at a crossing, try being ten feet under one! The thing finally got to the trestle with a roaring rumble that drowned out any attempt at speaking, and realizing we weren't going to die, we just sat there on the planks looking up and marveling at the iron belly of the beast. This went on for a few minutes, and when it was gone and the noise faded into the distance there was just a lot of silent staring.

After having escaped serious injury and/or death there was an important need for a profound statement to be made. Something that would sear the experience into our minds. Immortal words that would fly out into space and live forever, defining the life lesson we learned that fateful summer day. Finally, I spoke. "How cool was that, wanna wait for another one?"

Yeah, we decided that would be way cool, until the more logical kid among us mentioned how lucky we were nobody flushed the toilet as the train traversed the freaking trestle with us under it. Actually he did not use the word traversed, or freaking either, now that I think about it.

After quickly climbing down off the trestle we just continued our walk in the woods, which was anticlimactic at this point as there was nothing that could possibly scare or hurt us in the woods after what we had been through.

Other than perhaps Bootsy.

As soon as you start feeling and acting old...you are. Your attitude is the enemy not the calendar, geezer.

My recent trip to the dentist, not!

Billy meets Dr. Smith, the one dentist out of ten that recommends chewing sugary gum.

I have been hearing radio ads recently for a dentist who includes cheery jingles extolling the merits of good dental hygiene and regular checkups. It got me to thinking; it's about time for my regular dental checkup which at this point in my life is about, oh, every 30 years.

I have always had good teeth. I have my dad's teeth genetically speaking of course, and that's good. I also have his hair which is not so good as I grew out of it years ago, so in regards to the top of my head it makes for frosty freezy times in the winter and sun screen slathered sunny summer days. Given the choice, of which I had none, I pick good teeth. It is cheaper and less painful to care for hair no matter the follicle count, or lack of therein.

As a youngster other than having one rogue tooth pulled when I was five or six, visits to the dentist's office have not been particularly scary events. Check-ups consisted of the usual zero cavity clean bill of health and a sucker on the way out the door. Call it dental insurance, for the dentist. "Great teeth kid, keep it up…here, have a mouth full of sugar."

I went to the dentist for high school freshman check up in 1963 and as usual, no cavities, no problem. "Here kid, take this box of suckers and a couple cans of Coke..." Along about 1978 my thought was perhaps I should have the pearly off-whites checked just in case. Different dentist as the original one had retired a broken man having never had the opportunity to drill even one small hole in my head. Well of course after a 15 year absence from any dental care my mouth was full of...nothing but healthy teeth. I figured my decision in bumping up my teeth brushing frequency to 3-4 times a month must be paying off.

I helped the young dentist pay off his student loan by allowing him to give them a good cleaning, not that they needed it, and on the way out I ask for a sucker. He gave me an odd look and tossed me some peppermint floss.

I decided it would be advantageous to go every year if for nothing more than a good cleaning and conversation with the young dentist, and besides there is no risk as NOTHING is ever wrong with my teeth. So a year later I ride my motorcycle merrily to the tooth terminal and confidently open wide and say "av ak ick oc." Translation; "have at it doc." The garbled enunciation caused of course by trying to talk with my mouth open. Beer has also been known to cause me mispronunciation problems, and has the strangely similar effect of not allowing me to keep my mouth shut for more than a few seconds.

With confidence abounding I wait for the usual; "they're all fine, get your damn flavored floss and beat it". Only this time, and my teeth still sweat when I think about it, he says, "you have two cavities, do you want to take care of that today?"

You see I have this theory. I think he somehow planted cavity seeds or something in my mouth the year before and now it was time for the harvest, and I bet if I could have checked some phone records there would have been calls made to and from my old dentist. I suspect a conspiracy.

So we took care of it that day. My previously serene dental world was shattered by X-rays, Novocain shots, (it is true that only the first shot hurts, assuming of course you are dead by the time the second one is administered), and a high speed drill that sounded much like a small jet fighter trying to fly out of my nose. And yes the Novocain takes away any sensation that you are indeed drooling down your own chin and the front of your shirt, and it lasts for HOURS. This drooling thing is perfectly acceptable though at dental offices, and taverns where they know you – so I've heard - and of course the Supreme Court and CNN.

I started home a changed man wearing a slightly damp shirt. I'm sure some people would argue the point but my thought was; I don't think going to the dentist is much fun. So I made a mature, contemplative, and educated decision: I ain't going no more. Two cavities in one year after a lifetime of nothing...a coincidence? I think not. Dentist office, a grassy knoll in Dallas, it's all the same.

On the way home riding briskly along on my motorcycle that clear, bright and sunny day I think I was frowning though I can't be sure, but my cheeks were flapping merrily and uncontrollably in the breeze and drool was whisping smartly and copiously off my ears in a steady stream. The guy behind me in the pickup truck kept turning his windshield wipers off and on and looking up at the sky.

Yeah, I still feel bad about that.

I'm afraid I am becoming a very complex person, and I am just way too simple to handle it!

Little Johnny and the penny or; how Grandma went to jail.

Grandpa and Grandma invited their young grandson, Johnny, to spend the first month of his summer vacation with them on the farm. While visiting a local store Johnny found a little tractor in the toy aisle he wanted to buy, but had no money. Grandpa being kind hearted thought he would help the boy to purchase the tractor and also teach the lad some patience and how to handle money.

"Johnny," Grandpa said, "I will give you the money to buy the toy, but you will have to be patient as all good things in life take time to acquire and waiting for the things you really want can be a great virtue. Tell you what I'll do. I will give you a penny today, and if you are a good boy and help Grandma and me around the farm I will double the penny tomorrow then double the money again every day. Maybe by the end of the month you will have enough to buy your little toy tractor."

Johnny thought about this and concluded Grandpa was a cheapskate and living in the past when it comes to finances, but figured he would humor the old fart and free money is free money no matter how little the amount. "You promise to double my pennies every day?" Johnny asked his Grandpa, "I promise, every day." "Then it's a deal." Johnny said.

The old man handed the boy a penny and they went home and told Grandma about the arrangement. "That's nice." She said.

The next day after dinner Grandpa gave Johnny another penny, now he had money enough to jingle in his pocket, barely. On the third day he had four pennies rattling in his jeans, although he was thinking at this rate he would not have near enough money to get that toy tractor by the end of the month, but Grandpa was being very good about keeping his promise.

A week goes by and Grandpa has been steadily doubling the boy's money every day so on day seven he has a grand total of 32 cents. By the ninth day Grandpa says, "Whoa, we're over a whole dollar now, I will have to get you some pennies out of the jar on the dresser where I keep my loose change." Grandma didn't like the sound of this.

Grandpa began to grow a little un-easy as by the 14th day he had to ask Grandma to dip into her egg money as he owed Johnny $40.96. Now Johnny had his own jar on the dresser full of pennies. By the 17th day Grandpa had to cough up $327.68 in pennies. Grandma had no more egg money left so she had to sell a few chickens, and the sofa. "Stupid old fool." She said.

"Johnny, why don't we just go buy that little tractor today and maybe some more toys for you too." He inquired. "Then we can just call it even, okay?" "You promised." Johnny replied. "Besides, I have my eye on a MoPed now."

22 days into Johnny's lesson in patience and money management, and Grandpas rapid decent into Hell, he had to go into town and turn some savings into $10,485.76, worth of pennies and bring them back in the pickup truck in five bushel baskets. The boy now kept his stash of penny cash in the old coal bin in the basement, and was shopping for some high end flat screen HD TV equipment along with planning a two week stay at Disney World.

On day 25 the weary old man had sold his pick up truck along with two tractors and a combine, so he had the $83,886.08 in pennies delivered to the farm in a neighbor's grain truck. Johnny now had his sights set on a vintage Corvette and an entertainment center the size of Whoopi Goldberg's ego. Grandma was arrested on a street corner in town for attempted prostitution and selling poultry without a permit.

On day 29 the remainder of the farm machinery along with the house had been sold and the IRA drained. Johnny had rented a secured room in the bank as $1,342,177.28 worth of pennies takes up a lot of space. "Johnny, about that toy tractor...." Grandpa mumbled, his hands trembling. "You promised." Johnny replied. "Besides, I have my heart set on a Toy's-R-Us franchise and part ownership in a Hooters."

On the 30th day, which not coincidentally was the same day the remaining 400 acres of the farm were sold, and last day of the month, Johnny had the $2,684,354.56 in pennies shipped home in a rather large armored truck. He flew home in a leased private jet and was *really* grateful for the economic and virtue lessons he had learned from his Grandpa who by now only speaks the words, "Thirty days past September..." and, "A penny saved is a penny earned," though he does seem to enjoy humming Penny Lane while trying to stick table knives into electrical outlets at his new residence, Our Lady of the Perpetually Bewildered Rest Home.

Grandma still refers to him as that stupid old fool, and is currently on probation.

The morals of the story: The above will work best if Bill Gates is your Grandfather, as two and a half million dollars is probably his budget for Kleenex.

Grandpa was lucky there is only 30 days in June, or he might have had to come up with some serious cash and been ruined.

"Penny Lane" is a great old Beatles tune, and will now be stuck in your head for the next 27 hours.

Sometimes promises are only as good as your credit rating.

And, past the age of 65 there are certain things that you should not try to sell on the street. Poultry would be one of them.

I will not in any way ever violate my own personal moral principles, assuming of course that one day I may actually have some.

Give me some of that old time bean field religion!

Sometimes when men get together sooner or later we begin to compare scars and tell scary stories about how we got them. It's a guy thing, kind of our equivalent of women swapping birthing experiences, but the man-scar stories carry more significance and use less swear words.

One scary scar story revolves around a still noticeable scar on a finger of my right hand. Other scars I don't remember much about anymore, I do recall sitting on the pointy end of a lead pencil once but real men don't want to get that involved in scar show and tell.

I used to live in the country and one evening in the dead of winter a friend of mine whom I will call Jon, because that's his name, stopped in for a visit in his recently purchased blue $200 1950 Chevy. The long lane to the house was snow covered so he drove through the less snowy soybean field and got stuck.

And not just a little stuck, he had chains on the rear tires and apparently his logic was that if he spun the tires fast enough and long enough he would eventually get out. So there it sat with the back tires in two deep frozen dirt holes and the bumper almost touching the ground.

Next day Jon and I proceeded with the de-bean-fielding of the blue $200 1950 Chevy. We decided to jack the car up and put stout boards between the holes and the tires. He would then, in theory, be able to drive away.

I told Jon to slowly ease the clutch out while I lifted and pushed on the back bumper. This may have worked too except Jon for reasons known only to him and Satan popped the clutch and spun a board out from underneath the car at roughly twice the speed of sound where it rapidly decelerated against my gloved hand griping the bumper.

I know this might sound strange, but it hurt like hell! One of those full body, throbbing, nauseating pains that made the memory of the above mentioned pencil incident seem like a minor pain in the...past.

About this time a car stopped along the road by the entrance to the lane and a woman in a long coat began walking through the snow towards us. She arrived shortly after the supersonic board, which at that moment I had reason to believe might be the catalyst for my new future nickname of Stubby, had done its damage and without a greeting or introduction began reading something of a religious nature to us from a small pamphlet.

Oddly this coincided with my own religious awakening as I was saying some silent prayers that when I took off my glove the original set of fingers would still be intact.

In regards to the praying I know He initially heard me call His name as shortly after the impact I began shouting it very loudly although in a most non-religious manner. Jon's name was also brought up but was more of a statement regarding his apparent inability to follow simple instructions, his single digit IQ, and some reference was made to whether or not his parents were actually married at the time of his birth.

I slowly pulled the glove off and found everything still attached although the middle finger had a blood blister on it the size of a Volkswagen, and it was throbbing like the veins in Rosie O'Donnell's forehead after walking up a flight of stairs.

Between the pain and throbbing I was feeling woozy so I bent over to get some blood to my head. About this time the lady in the long coat seemed to pick up the tempo on her pamphlet reading, and as I went down on my knees to try and perhaps quell the growing feeling of nausea and dizziness I swear she gave out a hoot and a holler and a halleluiah!

Now Jon was apparently enjoying the unfolding drama as I could hear him laughing, and by the time I got faint enough to put my head down on the ground while kneeling and clasping my hands together I am pretty sure the pamphlet lady was speaking in tongues, rocking back and forth, trembling, and loosing bladder control.

Jon could be heard cackling hysterically like the demented devil worshipping illegally conceived trouble making clutch popper he really was.

By my actions in the bean field that day I know the pamphlet reading lady must have surely felt she was witnessing an instant convert to her religious order which the best I can figure is *The Church Of People In Long Coats Who Minister To Guys in Soybean Fields In The Dead Of Winter With Blue $200 1950 Chevy's Buried Up To Their Axles, Of Which One Guy Has A Blood Blister On A Smashed Middle Finger The Size Of A Volkswagen That Throbs Like The Veins In Rosie O'Donnell's Forehead After Walking Up A Flight of Stairs.*

I finally managed to pull myself off the ground, briefly showed her my injury, and then staggered up to the house to lie down for awhile.

She seemed extremely upset for some reason and stomped away, muttering something about *my* parental heritage and the need to change her underwear.

In retrospect I probably should have shown her more than just the one finger.

I win, you lose, it's nothing personal. Unless I lose...

The theory of pre-disaster or; do you smell smoke?

LOOKS LIKE IT'S GONNA BE A GOOD DAY.

In the 1982 movie, *The World According to Garp,* a realtor is showing the Robin Williams character Garp a beautiful house in the country. As they stand outside a small plane flies into view and crashes into the house tearing a big hole in it. "We'll take it." Garp says. After a protest from his wife, Garp tells her: "Don't you see, this house has been *Pre-Disastered*! Nothing else bad can ever happen to it!"

I race a formula car, a Formula Vee to be specific, in road racing events with *Midwestern Council of Sports Car Clubs* (MC) and *Sports Car Club of America* (SCCA). Other than try to explain in detail what that is all about, just think of the type of car Danica Patrick has driven in the Indy 500. The difference being that I am of course a faster driver and our drivers suits fit differently in different places.

I first became aware of my own racing related Pre-Disaster connection some years ago while towing my enclosed race car trailer with a small motor home to the first race of the season at my favorite place on earth, *Blackhawk Farms Raceway* near Rockton IL (Patrick's home town is the nearby Roscoe) I went just a tad too fast across an intersection with a couple of humps in it, and the ensuing combination of scraping and banging told me my trailer had indeed come loose. Upon inspection of the trailer I found the electrical wiring had been ground in half, the bottom of the hitch was much flatter than I remembered, and there was a rather large hole in the aluminum skin of the trailer made by the hitch on the motor home.

"Bleep!" says I. "I haven't even gotten to the bleep'n track and already things are going to bleep'n hell! For the love of Mario Andretti what the bleep is going to happen next...BLEEP!!"

After doing a little wrench work to adjust the 2 inch hitch to better accommodate what turned out to be a 1-7/8 inch ball...BLEEP! I was successfully on my way with out the burden of worrying about functioning turn signals, tail or stop lights on the trailer.

After this disaster I did not figure on much success in regards to racing as the tow went so badly, but the rest of the weekend was great and I actually won my very first Formula Vee race, so everything did not turn out so bleep'n bad after all, and thus the concept of being Pre-Disastered began to emerge.

Now, there are varying degrees of Pre-Disaster situations that at least for me seem to produce results. At first it was just kind of a funny line to tell people in regards to various misfortunes before a race. "Hey, had a trailer tire blowout on the way here, beat the liv'n bleep out of the wheel well, had to bang the sheet metal back into place with a rubber hammer, on the interstate...in the rain. I'm Pre-Disastered, ha, ha, probably going to win the race!

And did.

A nice easy Pre-Disaster is a simple loss of trailer hub caps. Not much of a disaster really but seems to produce favorable results. To this point I have lost seven or eight cheap plastic ones in three different states, so I am thinking this particular Pre-Disaster is a cumulative thing.

The trailer falling off the jack in the yard worked pretty well, along with the exhaust system on the motor home coming apart. Once the canopy on the motor home took it upon itself to start un-rolling before we got to the track, and a couple of spark plug wires came off that same vehicle on one trip, but I won the two races.

At a summer race weekend heading to Blackhawk Farms, we were in a stretch of road construction and went over a big bump which got me to wondering if I had remembered to secure all the latch points on the trailer door/ramp. The nice people passing us and gesturing frantically towards the back of the trailer confirmed that I apparently had not. After stopping and putting that back in order the smoke coming from under the dash of the motor home caught our attention and had to be dealt with, something to do with having the emergency flashers shorting out or some such thing. Burning wires put out some really acrid smoke, but later I smoked 'em on the track and won the race.

On the subject of smoke, during a spring time tow to a race at Autobahn Country Club near Joliet, IL the girlfriend and I were a few miles from the track and commenting that someone must have a camp or brush fire going as it was most fragrant, and seemed to be getting more fragrant as we rolled along. Just to make sure we weren't on fire or some impossibly stupid thing like that, I turned around to look in the back of the camper and saw the unit was filling up with a lot of bleep'n smoke. I said to her with a none too measured amount of calmness delivered in a rather high pitch, "that's not outside, that's us! BLEEP...BLEEP!!"

After stopping, quickly, and running around the motor home in a barely controlled panic, I determined the smoke was coming from under the refrigerator, and had a few small flames still licking at a hole burned in some plywood. (Bad propane gas regulator) Being nothing if not innovative, I quenched the fire with a spray bottle of Windex, which not only ended the Pre-Disaster but also left the bottom of the frig streak free. Won the race in the rain, and the motor home is now known with reverence and contempt, as "Old Smoky,"

Now, I'm not saying all this pre-race drama always guarantees really good results or a win every time. For example, after pulling out of the driveway on the way to a double race weekend with SCCA I noticed some familiar yet unwelcome scraping and banging as I had forgot to snap the latch down on the ball of the hitch. By the time I slowed and stopped after dragging the trailer by its safety chains through the local business district, I had *three* nice new yet not particularly neatly punched holes in the front of the trailer.

One theory from this incident is the Pre-Disaster gods presented me with a trailer hole for each of the two races coming up that weekend, and one for luck. Another theory is that I am just a feckless idiot. Anyway I got a 3rd and a 4th.

Chatting with a fellow competitor at that event I asked if he had a spare nose to put on his car, a Formula Ford as in the previous practice session he had spun in front of me on the track and I ran over his original one, while still attached to his race car, crunching it like a cracker. I believe this gentleman is working on his own version of race Pre-Disaster and I am always willing to help a fellow racer. He won his race class.

I'm not sure if this race Pre-Disaster phenomena is my secret weapon or not, however I don't think it can be artificially created by beating the hell out of ones equipment on purpose, although I seriously believe all the other competitors in my Formula Vee race class should give that a try and let me know how it works. In fact I would be willing to give them a bleep'n hand.

If I ever end up racing alongside Danica surely my trailer is lying dead in a ditch somewhere. And if I were to be ahead of her it could only mean, sadly, that Old Smokey has finally burned to the ground.

Oh, and if you find my hubcaps, I want them back.

Road racing makes heroin addiction look like a vague wish for something salty.

Peter Egan

The night of the Metal Munching Monster...the horror...the horror...

THE SCENE: Sometime in the early middle of a July night in a 26 foot motor home parked at the Road America road racing course outside Elkhart Lake, WI.

SHE, with a note of urgency and emotion in her voice: *"There' something knawing on the outside of the motor home!"*

ME, with no emotion: *"No, there's not."*

SHE, more excited now: *"I'm telling you there's something out there doing something to the motor home!"*

ME, equaling the previously mentioned emotion: *"Go to sleep."*

SHE: *"I definitely hear something making chewing and grinding noises out there!"*

ME: ....

THE SCENE: Sometime in the late middle of the same night, same place.

SHE, with great urgency: *"Wake up, that thing is still out there chewing on metal. I can hear it and feel it!"*

ME, initiating my sleepy sarcasm mode: *"Give me a shout when it finally has a hole chewed all the way through."*

SHE, with a touch of anger in her voice now, presumably brought upon by unappreciated sleepy sarcasm: *"Not funny! There's something out there! Go see what it is!"*

MY INNER MONOLOGUE: I have to get up in a couple of hours and prepare to be a hero race driver in a Midwestern Council of Sports Car Clubs event and I am not getting much sleep at this point. There *was* this nice little poster at race registration listing some of the local wild life populating the track area, know killers such as turtles, raccoons, chipmunks, deer, turkeys, and I know there are badgers in the area, Wisconsin is the Badger State after all. They are not particularly bright animals so many of them have run for public office and become quite influential in state politics.

Badgers can be nasty little cusses but no mention was made verbally or in the supplemental regulations of any deficiencies in the local badgers diet that might lead them to ingest aluminum and/or steel in the form of race car support vehicles, and I think this would have at least been brought up in passing by the track management.

I suppose it's possible but not probable that a deranged badger, badger, we don't need no stinking badger, could be out there chewing away on the aluminum motor home skin for some reason, and I can tell by the tone of her voice SHE is really scared and not going to be able to get any sleep (me neither) if in her mind SHE's absolutely sure something huge, heinous and horrendously destructive to man and machine is trying to burrow its way into the motor home.

I can most certainly understand her terror as whatever she perceives to be eating its way through a combination of about an inch of aluminum and wood could do some deathly damage to human tissue and bone, and in its rampage leave bloody body parts strewn all over the ground and tossed upon overturned race cars!

ME, taking into account the genuinely frightening experience SHE has endured for a good part of this long and for her, terrifying night, and with much compassion in my voice I say: *"Leave me alone."*

SHE, with great agitated expectation: *"I'm telling you there is something outside trying to eat its way inside! Get up and go see what it is!!"*

ME, realizing now any hope for another hour or two of sleep has all but evaporated unless closure comes to this issue: *"Let me get this straight. You say there is some kind of metal munching monster out there, trying to eat its way in here, supposedly to make us into either a late night snack or early breakfast, depending on its time of arrival."*

SHE: *"Yes."*

ME: *"And you will not accept me saying there's nothing out there?"*

SHE: *"No."*

ME: *"So, you want me to get up and go outside in the dark wearing nothing but my "Just Shut Up And Drive" tee-shirt, standard issue blue with little red stripes briefs, and genuine authentic made in China Indian moccasins, and chase off or do battle with whatever is out there that you are sure eats metal, and if this apparently super natural being does actually exist it will certainly tear me limb from limb, and what ever parts it doesn't eat will probably scatter from the front straight to at least turn six, is this correct?"*

SHE: *"Better take a flashlight."*

ME: *"Right."*

You can't argue with a woman's logic. It is easier to just skip merrily along into the Valley of Death and hope for the best.

So I get up, grab a flashlight, unlock the door and step outside to find...ALL THE OTHER CAMPERS WITH GREAT JAGGED HOLES IN THEM, TENTS TORN TO SHREDS, AND BLODDY BODY PARTS STREWN ALL OVER THE GROUND AND TOSSED UPON OVERTURNED RACE CARS!!

Maybe that was a bit exaggerated. Actually it was just a dark almost predawn night with a gentle breeze, and although I did give some thought to throwing myself against the motor home and screaming as a little joke, I did not want to be faced with the prospect of having to make my own breakfast.

Standing in the dark, yawning from excitement, my ears not very desperately searching for the frightening sound of ripping metal, I spied the beast and immediately leap into action.

After a brief confrontation I quickly overcame the thing and returned to the safety and comfort of the motor home.

SHE: *"What was it? What was it?"*

ME, trying to speak through the adrenaline rush that comes from mortal combat: *"You had every reason to be scared, but fear not, I have met on the field of battle this morn and claim victory over the dreaded indigenous <u>Road America Camping Permit Tag</u>, and although it repeatedly attacked the vehicle by sliding back and forth with much fervor on the rear view mirror bracket, it failed by every measure to breech our aluminum armored fortress, and yea, I say unto you at this moment it is held fast and secure by duct tape to the aforementioned bracket...you happy now?"*

SHE muttered something somewhat incoherent but if I remember correctly there was a crudely worded reference to and accusation of me being akin to an intelligent donkey. I believe there also was some question as to legitimacy of my birth.

I might just as well thrown myself screaming against the motor home just for fun per my original thought, as breakfast was indeed self served, cold and quiet.

Note: There were no Road America Camping Permit Tags or stinking badgers harmed in the above incident.

Brakes, if used properly in a race car, are commonly only needed to stop and pick up the checkered flag for your victory lap.

I'm telling ya, there ain't no dog in that dog house.

A while back on my way home from a very rainy racing weekend competing with SCCA, Sports Car Club of America, I was driving south on Interstate 39 in the motor home pulling the trailer housing my Formula Vee, and with the sky brightening and the outside temperature warming up it was a gorgeous late afternoon. With no wind and the cruise control set I was quite enjoying the drive after having a successful although cool and wet race in the rain earlier in the day at Blackhawk Farms Raceway.

Of course this couldn't last.

The motor home started slowing and surging which was telling me the big old 440 V8 was on the fritz. I pulled off at the next ramp and removed the engine cover or in the lexicon of motor-homing, the "dog house" which did not have any trace of a dog in it, that is between the front seats. The motor idled and revved up just fine then, of course, but I decided to take two lane highways the rest of the maybe 50 miles home just to be sure I did not get stranded on the interstate.

By this time I figured it was a fuel pump problem and as I was at one time a Boy Scout whose motto is, "Be prepared, always carry a spare fuel pump," I had a new one with me. Not wanting to change it out on the highway I was going to try and limp home, but it was slow going.

After a few miles the speed went from 50 to 40 and painfully down to about 15 mph. I made the decision to try and replace the fuel pump; tools were not a problem as I had most everything I own in the trailer. About the time it was barely running at all I came across a nice little rest area with paved roads and parked it.

Now the motor home is over thirty years old and the blessed automotive technology of the time was to mount the fuel pump on the front of the motor where God and the Chrysler Corporation decreed it should be, not buried in a gas tank as most are nowadays and therefore easier to work on by pseudo mechanics like me. Unfortunately one rusty threaded fitting would not come loose without twisting and probably breaking the fuel line, and I was not looking forward to spending any quality time with an AAA certified tow truck driver, so I took off again hoping for the best.

Within a few more miles the motor was running so badly that it actually stalled a couple of times on the highway. It would start again but barely move. The motor just simply was not getting enough gas.

Then suddenly the iconic yet cartoonish light bulb blinked on over my head. I had accidently hit a dome light switch with my elbow, but oddly about that same time I had a bold, brilliant, and deliciously chancy idea that will either get me home or maybe a picture and a couple of paragraphs in the local news paper under the headline: "Fiery Tragedy Strikes Moron In Motor Home. Dog Missing."

I removed the dog house with still no sign of any dog and lifted off the top of the air cleaner which exposed the carburetor less than three feet away from where I sit. I got an empty plastic Coke Zero bottle, dumped water out of two other plastic bottles, drilled very small holes in the caps and filled them with race car gas.

The rest of the successful trip home was spent driving with one hand while pouring gas into the carburetor with the other. Actually I found the motor did not respond favorably to either the pouring or squirting of copious amounts of gas down its throat as the ensuing backfiring through the carburetor was very attention getting as any sane person would expect with a foot and a half of blue flame shooting up ones forearm. About that time I was surprised to hear someone screaming like a little girl, turned out to be me.

Not that I do, but if I would be in the habit of shaving the hair on my arms, I would not have to bother with the right one for at least a couple of weeks. A dribble of Coke Zero tainted gas every now and then seemed to do the trick. Of course with the hot engine opened up to the inside of the motor home, the interior temp stayed a fairly balmy 103 degrees for most of the way home.

I did manage to avoid the picture and paragraphs in the local paper and have yet to find any trace of that dog, gave some thought to shaving the hair on my left forearm though but ended up just using a propane torch to get just the right match.

Should not those who are forever bleating about how we should be more tolerant to all, be more tolerant of the intolerant?

WARNING: Some smoking may occur.

THE LOLLIPOP GUILD BETWEEN TAKES

I was sitting at the computer some time back half watching and listening to the TV, when a promotion came on about a new movie soon to be released. Wasn't paying much attention until they got to the rating and warnings part, and what caught my ear at the very end was the discloser that some scenes contained - brief smoking.....

I had never heard this one before. Amazing, the Hollywood geniuses who provide us with good wholesome movie fare often involving sometimes as much as four consecutive words strung together before somebody says &%$#, or *@*&#~, and more bloodletting in two hours than the Red Cross can accomplish in a year, is now concerned we may be affected or offended by watching people smoke in a movie.

If this new rating goes retroactive more old films than not will need this warning, other than maybe the Wizard of Oz although I would wager even the Munchkins were smoke'n 'em if they had 'em between takes. Cutting out all smoking scenes from old movies would make them an average of 14 minutes long and you would never see Humphrey Bogart again.

I have to confess here that even I used to smoke cigarettes but kicked that nasty ash tray breath habit, at the age of nine.

I grew up with two smoking parents which was not uncommon way back when doctors were hyping one coffin nail brand or another in advertisements; indeed we had doctor recommended cigarettes. Of course back in the 50's we also had those really pointy bras that could put an eye out if the wearer bumped into someone of less than average height, so there was more than enough smoking related insanity and accidental blindness to go around.

My sister smoked and I felt the need to act mature so I started bumming half smoked cigarettes off her and puff away, not inhale mind you, just puff. Come on, I was nine! Spent a week in Chicago with her and of course wanted to light up far from the disapproving smoke clouded eyes of my parents, and I was obliged big time.

She gave me my own carton of smokes for the stay and I was in smoked ham hog heaven, but with the caveat that I now had to inhale as this was what *real* smokers do. This I did and about two and a half cigarettes later the scene could have been rated NVM (Not Very Mature) as I lay prone on the couch watching the ceiling rotate and convulsed in great moaning with my forearm over my increasingly green forehead feeling like I was surely on my way to human heaven, which at that point would have been welcomed.

My sister, God bless her, made me a confirmed non-cigarette smoker before I even grew out of my Mickey Mouse ears.

I have been bemused since then with the strange allure of inhaling smoke, the occasional campfire, leaf burning, and parking lot burnout aside. As I watched a friend many years ago when we were both barely teenagers teach himself to smoke with much tearing of eye and coughing, I asked if he was having fun. I think his reply was something like: "Arrack...bleeurk...harrkk...sncraaaaakkle...llrrrmm...umph," which is beginning smoker-speak for; "I believe my left lung is lodged in my larynx."

I have imagined a scenario where someone awakens to their house on fire, and with great choking and coughing they crawl on the floor through rancid smoke and heat, barely escaping with their life. While outside slumped against a tree watching the smoke and flames waiting for the fire department, they light up a cigarette, take a big drag and exclaim; "Wow, that was a close call...harrkk!"

But I for one get a warm fuzzy feeling all over knowing the entertainment industry people care enough to warn me of this particular celluloid and video ugliness involving actors smoking on screen. This way I can be forewarned and avert my eyes and not let it taint and spoil the rest of the flick and maybe make pale the usual amount of bad *%#@*!& language, or any on-screen depiction of maniacal chain saw mutilation, body ripping explosion, senseless killing, general bad behavior and mayhem, or the most vile thing movie makers can subject the audience to – full nude-al frontity...no wait, I like that part. But what will be next, a warning there may be brief scenes of Big Mac's or Buffalo wings being scarfed down...or excessive donut consumption? There go the cop shows.

Certainly cigarettes are bad for you, but with all the real trouble and conflict going on in the world do the Hollywood elite and watchdog ratings mavens now feel that even *watching* smoking on screen is damaging to one's health and well being? Caution: Rated PR for *Pretty Ridiculous.*

Regardless of the entertainment industry's influence we turned the corner years ago by banning most cigarette advertisements which has surely saved many lungs and lives. We have also been able to prevent serious eye injuries in a lot of short statured people by wisely adapting the basic pointy bra design technology into the manufacture of silly party hats and Sno-Cone cups. "I'll have a Pineapple flavored cone in a Double D please."

Don't Bogart that butt, Munchkin.

Was at the store today, the girl behind the counter said, "have a nice day!" "Too late," said I, "already watched the news and bought gas."

Deer motorist,

In the fall of the year we celebrate Halloween and oft times we have to tolerate elections, both scary events the former in a fun way and the latter in a not so fun way, but both involving a large number of frightening creatures holding out their bags and demanding either candy or cash. At least the candy seekers are cute, reasonably intelligent and have some idea what they are doing.

Something else scary in the fall time of year is deer rut season in Illinois and wherever else these killer Bambi's reside.

Driving a small sports car alongside a wooded hill over 30 years ago I had my first deer encounter. All the warning I had was a quick peripheral flash and then the "whomp." Those of you having met deer on the highway in this manner are familiar with the sound.

Luckily the now dead deer in question was not very large so the car was still drivable although a bit hard to see forward over the big bulge now in the hood. I drove back into the nearby town to report the strike, and then proceeded on what promised to be a long drive home as the deer impact had punctured a hole in the radiator. So it was drive a bit, shut it off to cool, drive a bit, shut it off to cool... Finally got to the next town and found a gentlemen working late in his motorcycle shop who carved up a wooden dowel which was driven into the hole with a hammer. As this was a British sports car it was probably an improvement over the original design. After topping off the radiator with water I proceeded home with no difficulties, in fact drove it like that for a couple of weeks until the proper repair was made.

In the years that have followed I have personally had many, many sighting and close encounters of the deer/car kind, including having the side of a police cruiser in which I was riding caved in by a deer never even seen until we looked back after the "whomp" and saw it lying on the highway amidst flying fur. And by the way it was not an official transportation to and from situation, it was a ride along with a county deputy, no matter what the rumors were and the police report said.

I have gone side by side down a road a few times with deer as I blew the horn and yelled, "Don't turn left! Don't turn left! And after spending two years restoring another sports car I missed hitting one of those rats with antlers by maybe 30 feet. This was about April 1992 and out of curiosity I started keeping track of deer accidents reported in the local paper from that point on until the end of the year, about nine months. The count was near 100. This does not include unreported incidents, near misses, or car theft by drunken joy riding deer.

The point I am trying to make is: There are just too many damn deer.

A lot of people feel this way and yet others think they are beautiful, delicate, and graceful creatures of the woodland. A sub-group of the delicate and graceful contingent are those that used to think that way, until they hit a deer. And for those not so afflicted, yet, with automotive deer rash I always try to have them imagine propping up a 150 pound sandbag on 4 two by fours and driving into it going 55-60 miles an hour, then compare the afore mentioned delicate concept to the reality of "whomp."

Deer are just plain stupid and are often times desensitized to vehicles and traffic. While driving by a pasture I once observed six or seven less than 50 yards off the roadway just lounging around drinking beer, so I turned into the field and commenced with great horn blowing and motor revving to get them to move farther away from the road. They just calmly looked at me all doe eyed....but kept on lying there; I think some of them were smoking. I gave some thought to driving onto the posted farm field and chasing them but wanted to keep my experience of police cruiser riding to the front seat and not the back.

So I have no use what so ever for deer. I am always watchful of areas where they might be, which is EVERYWHERE! I have even had wait in line behind them at the liquor store. This watchfulness has helped keep the sheet metal on my vehicles smooth and shiny, and I have chosen to rarely if ever ride a motorcycle after dark as I am a big self preservationist chicken.

I am not a hunter, having given that up years ago after coming to grips with the, *if you shoot it you have to dress it and eat it,* concept. Much easier to keep my appetite intact and just order up a cheeseburger. But I say GO DEER HUNTERS! Without them there would be a lot more deer carcasses, shattered car parts, beer cans, and half smoked cigarettes lying along the road.

Years ago our roads were safer when it came to deer accidents because there just plain were not that many in the area. Deer hunters then had to travel to different states to take a crack at them, now I know of people who stand on their back porch in the country and bag one of these four footed forces of evil before breakfast. Way back if you saw a deer around here at all it was something special. Of course it can be argued that seeing a deer in your headlights 1.3 seconds before you slam into it is pretty special too, but more in a busted car and insurance claims sort of way.

We need more of these pests harvested! Interesting term, harvesting, as it relates to deer. Extrapolating the word would lead us to believe that farmers in the fall of the year may be in fact, shooting corn.

To reduce the deer population how about lengthening the various hunting seasons, upping limits, and maybe creating more seasons. As long as deer are meandering around on the roads anyway, how about a "Weld A Spear to the Front Of Your Pickup Truck," season, Maybe "Machine Gun a Deer from an Airplane," season." Variants on these could also be useful around election time for controlling those other pests.

There would still be plenty of work for auto body shops for sure and increased business for the meat processors, plus it would help keep my sports cars from getting all wrinkly in the front. So shoot more deer, less corn. One final word. Whomp.

Humans trying to stop global climate change is much akin to fleas trying to stop the dog from shedding.

Dear Al,

Dear Al Gore,

Just thought I would drop you a line while sitting outside here camping in the woods. As you are the global warming, I'm sorry, "climate change" guru, I just wanted to let you know that it is a bit past the middle of July here in the Midwest and as I write this at 7 in the evening it is all of 56 degrees and is supposed to dip into the mid 40's later before dawn. I am wearing shorts as I refuse to give into the not-very-global-warming-like chill, and well, I'm afraid I have frozen one of my cojones off. I will enclose it with this correspondence.

   I of course don't know where you will be when this letter, and small box catches up to you but if history follows course you may be speaking at some venue on the dangers of global warming...there I go again, climate change, and it will probably be snowing. I don't know why, and I am sure you don't have a clue either, but it seems like most every time I hear you are speaking, well bleating actually, about the perils we have from the earth's climate warming up, or whatever the heck you think it is doing that you are able to scare the bejesus out of people about, the weather is cold and oft times blizzard-like. Huh, seems kinda odd and counter intuitive, does it not!

Of course you could just be sitting around your really large house with all the lights on filling out forms for more carbon credits that you can handily afford for said house and the pollution spewing private jets you seem to have an affinity for. Or you could be composing some treatise on how we out here in carbon spewing private jet flyover land need to be very, very concerned about outdoor grilling or mowing the lawn with a gas power mower or flatulent bovines or some such other noble and yet embarrassingly stupid idea you and the other morons, whoops, junk scientists, whoops again, brilliant academic minds can convolute to help avert a global disaster that you would have us believe will happen on the third Monday of next month unless we buy your stupid movie and book.

But then again it does give the citizenry a pretty gosh darn good idea on your mental makeup, aloofness, and just how stupid you think we really are.

But heck, who am I to criticize, in the popular and profitable global warming industry you are making millions on the simple, and I know you are familiar with simple, concept of scaring people to death with your, how do I say it gracefully, bag full of global warming bovine gas.

I have to agree with you however that the climate is changing; this has been a constant from the beginning of the earth's existence. Although more and more scientists, you know, the ones who actually study these things without an agenda in mind and are not on your payroll or trying to peddle their own agenda driven books, would tell you if you would take the royalty checks out of your ears and listen that if anything the earth is cooling.

I know you don't want to hear this and as it is detrimental to your income and maybe a pin in your inflated self image balloon, not to mention being a threat to future ways in which the government intends to bleed the taxpayers even more, but if my chilly fingers now struggling on this July evening to put pen to paper are any indication those real scientists may be right!

Oh golly, I had the radio turned down low but just heard something on the news about the lowest temps ever recorded in Tennessee in the month of July, right around where you live actually. Makes me think you may be bleating in your own front yard.

Better dress in layers, this global warming business may put you at risk for frostbite and perhaps some body parts falling off, and try not to let the audience, you know, the ones wearing snow boots and parkas in your yard there, see your breath in the chill...

Well I better get inside and light up a can of Sterno to try and keep from freezing the other...whoops...too late. Gonna need a bigger box.

The problem with being too open minded is the danger of your brains falling out.

On intelligent design: This goo is for you.

HOW GOD CREATED ADAM

Evolution versus Intelligent Design (ID), it is a topic that pops up in the news and is debated often among individuals. The ID concept has lately been highly touted by students and faculty of *The Divine School of Evolution Sucks,* wherein they believe all life including human life as we know it has been in some way designed by something or someone with great intelligence and has not just evolved. They are certain we are the product of a maker.

The hard core proponents of evolution, many of whom have graduated with honors from *Missing Link University* (Berkley) would have you believe all life including we humans came from a puddle of very pre-historic, pre-everything goo that just randomly somehow turned into extremely simple and barely functional life forms (scientific term: Congress) and then evolved into humans, kind of. Normally when questioned on how this could come about they would tell you, "It just happened, probably on a Tuesday." Fair enough. Some people don't want to be bothered with giving a long convoluted explanation they have no chance of ever themselves understanding or explaining to others. Kind of like when women try to explain their feelings to men. A man's usual response to that attempt: "Yeah honey, I think I understand now. Uh, could you move out of the way a bit, their lining up to try for the extra point."

Just for amusement purposes let's imagine a simple recreation of an evolutionary process. First we need a recipe. We start with an amount of iron ore, some bauxite, sand, copper, carbon, and maybe some bits and pieces of gold and silver. Then some wood and various other fibrous type materials including perhaps rubber plants and cotton, and don't forget to add one of the mainstays of modern life, silicone.

Now, put them in a pit of some sort, perhaps spray the stuff with petroleum, leave it alone and wait. How long will we have to wait, and what are we waiting for? Well give it at least several thousand years, actually a million would be better, and pure evolution being what it is purported to be we can expect that out of that pit eventually will come an F-16 fighter plane, maybe a Lexus, or a wide screen digital HDTV or an IPod, at the very least a simple computer chip should evolve, right?

All the basic materials needed are in the mix for one or more of the above to come into existence, iron ore for steel, bauxite for aluminum, sand for glass, cotton for a Tee-shirt that says "Evolution Sucks," on the front, and of course silicon to help fill out the Tee-shirt. Presumably with enough time and maybe the right temperature, something should "just happen."

Well it's not going to just happen. If the above were possible then eventually toaster ovens, electric cars, and lap top computers will be sprouting out of the ground from junk yard and landfills everywhere like high-tech electro-mechanical watermelons. Actually I think that is the origin of electric cars.

Those items need a designer, someone to take the raw materials and fashion them into the useful things they eventually will become. Someone to create, to mold, to explain to the little woman exactly how import that extra point can be and why she should not stand in front of the TV during those critical moments.

Yes, it takes an intelligent mind and a skilled hand to make stuff and make stuff work. We humans are very capable of designing and developing simple and complex items along with fine works of art and literary masterpieces. Along the way we have developed our human intelligence and reasoning powers to an astounding degree, the current administration and Hollywood notwithstanding.

As "things" have been designed, so have we. There is way too much complexity in just the workings of the human brain, body, and soul, let alone the rest of the natural world, to believe it all came about because of a random yucky coagulation of raw materials millions of years ago. Who and what we are now came about through the work and blessing of the most highly intelligent entity, greatest thinker and most important being in the universe, the savior of us all. That's right, Barack Hussein Obama. Go ahead, ask him.

The thought of any remotely human-like life form coming from some primordial puddle of goo is just ridicules.

Well okay maybe Congress.

We're from the government and here to help you.

To Serve Man... "It's a cookbook!"

Twilight Zone episode: 1962

Of silly laws, moose, and dumb dogs.

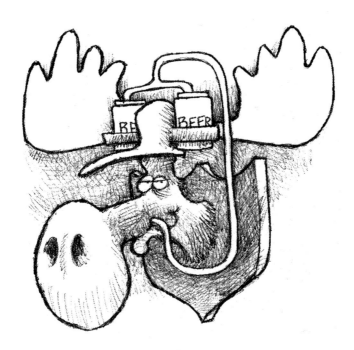

The biggest problem with the legislative process is that we elect legislators, lawmakers to, well, make laws, and frankly this has been a bane on our society since the founding of this nation. It is necessary to some reasonable extent of course but a good lawmaker is one that actually makes very few or no laws at all, although after getting elected most feel they are obligated to come up with some kind of law no matter how ridiculous and silly that law might be. Other legislators will then jump on the dumb-ass wagon and pass the bill into law because many of them possess less common sense than dried dog crap.

To get an idea of the sublime and the ridiculous things lawmakers have come up with in the past here are a few actual examples from various states, and no I am not making this up.

In Alabama "it is illegal for a driver to be blindfolded while operating a vehicle." The way some people drive around here I'm pretty sure that's legal in Illinois. Also "it is illegal to wear a fake mustache that causes laughter in church." Well then what's the point or fun in going to church in Alabama? And "it is illegal to drive the wrong way down a one-way street if you have a lantern attached to the front of your automobile." Additional penalties will be assessed if you are wearing a fake mustache and headed to church.

In Alaska they are very protective of their moose population as "moose may not be viewed from an airplane," "it is considered an offense to push a live moose out of a moving airplane," and "it is considered an offense to feed alcoholic beverages to a moose." My thought is that if a moose can't hold his liquor when flying he deserves to be pushed out of an airplane, especially if he is sitting in coach, as nobody likes to watch the buffoonery of an intoxicated moose anyway, it just encourages them.

In Arizona "hunting camels is prohibited" but apparently this state does not disallow getting them drunk and pushing them out of airplanes, and in the spirit of fairness "when being attacked by a criminal or burglar you may only protect yourself with the same type of weapon that the other person possesses..." So I presume if a burglar entering your premises is not armed at all you can't even engage him in a pillow fight but are allowed to follow him home and burglarize *his* house.

In California "it is a misdemeanor to shoot at any kind of game from a moving vehicle unless the target is a whale." (Insert Michael Moore joke here.) Bombing one from an airplane with a bombed moose might work even better and could teach the moose a valuable behavioral lesson. I'm not sure what lesson the whale would learn, exactly. And "nobody is allowed to ride a bicycle in a swimming pool," well there goes my California vacation plans. "Persons classified as "ugly" may not walk down any street," and if caught will be sent to Wisconsin where it is perfectly legal. "It is illegal to pile horse manure more than 6 feet high on a street corner," but puts no restrictions on how high it can be piled in the state legislature.

Speaking of horses, Colorado says "it is illegal to ride a horse while under the influence." I figure if a horse buys his own drinks he can get as liquored up as he wants.

In Connecticut "you may not educate dogs." So that's why their state motto is, "Connecticut, Land of Really Stupid Dogs."

Florida law states, "if an elephant is left tied to a parking meter, the parking fee has to be paid just as it would for a vehicle." That's only fair; I always feed the meter when I tie my elephant to it as he does takes up more room than Michael Moore after a free buffet. "It is considered an offense to shower naked."...ah...but, if you're not...oh never mind.

It is illegal in Georgia "to use profanity in front of a dead body which lies in a funeral home or any coroners office." I'm just guessing here but I assume it is okay to swear like a scalded Baptist if they are dead and *standing* in a funeral home or coroner's office. "Signs are required to be written in English." Uh.............

Idaho has a law that says "it is illegal for a man to give his sweetheart a box of candy weighing less than 50 pounds. They must've meant potatoes, not candy...for the love of Oprah, they had to mean potatoes!

In Illinois "it is illegal to give a dog whiskey." Damn straight, make him pay for it like they do the horses in Colorado.

If you don't stand for something you'll lay down for everything.

My cat the terrorist.

When I lived in the country I owned a dog and a few cats. Actually you never really own a cat; you are just a large bipedal annoyance they put up with because you feed them. Originally there was one cat that wandered onto the place, a pretty cat it was with one blue eye and one yellow. And female as the one cat before very long turned into the above mentioned few, as cats will do. I ended up just calling her Mother Cat. She was well fed and taken care of, although I'm sure being a typical cat she would dispute this, even as she munched on a fine gourmet selection of *Only Really Starving Cats Would Eat this Crap* brand cat food.

One spring day I noticed she was slowly crawling out on a tree limb about 10 feet off the ground. She was making her way towards a Robin nest with baby birds in occupation.

Mother Cat had become a Bird Terrorist. It's a cat thing apparently.

I was more liberal back then so I figured the best thing to do is go talk to, yes I said talk to the cat. I climbed the tree to the Branch of Bird Terror, slid out a few feet and tapped her on the back. I may have said something like, "excuse me, we need to talk." She turned around with a calm yet bemused, "why is he bothering me when I have something to kill" look and laid down on the limb no doubt annoyed that I was going to make her late for her dinner date with the Robin family.

So there I was on a ten foot high limb attempting to reason and negotiate with an animal whose spends the better part of its day licking its crotch and hacking up a fur balls.

I explained to her she had no reason going after those innocent birds as she was well fed and I felt she was just doing this for the thrill of killing and whatever vendetta, real or imagined she had against birds. She should just come on down from the branch, let them live in peace and not leave them in pieces, and if she did I would give her some of those nice stinky cat treats she liked, or money.

She seemed to listen patiently and intently so in my liberal and therefore predominantly illogical mind at the time I assumed I had made my point and she would call off the attack and vacate the tree. As I was sliding back down the limb she calmly turned around and headed back towards the nest. At this point I reach out and gave Mother Cat a good liberal swat that propelled her maybe fifteen feet away from the tree. I think I might have called out her name or some variation of it right before hand met fur.

Factoring in the height of the branch and the horizontal arc, I make it near 30 feet of floundering feline flight. It is true what they say about a cat flying or falling though the air; they indeed almost always hit the ground, and no she never again attempted a kitty jihad against birds in that tree.

So much for trying to reason and negotiate with someone/something bent on terrorizing and killing, for whatever reason. Me thinks many in government could learn a lot from the above story as it relates to their approach in dealing with terrorist and other sub-human animals worldwide who clearly need to be swatted out of existence. How about chasing this bunch of politicians – many of whom are more disposed to apologizing to the evil people of this world than stopping them - up a really big tree occupied by a gaggle of rabid terrorist types looking to have some fun while avenging...oh whatever, and see if they could *reason* and *negotiate* their way safely back down before the guns, knives and fur balls came out, or the impatient and more than fed up citizenry chopped down the tree.

Best be keep'n your voting axes sharpened.

This is a test of the Emergency Alert System. Are you alert? Yeah that's what I thought.

Needful things.

There are a few things we just can't live without, and when I say we of course I mean me. Your list may vary but technology and four easy payments on your credit card have provided us with many gotta have 'em items.

Cruise control: Best automotive accessory since fuzzy dice. I have driven a lot of miles without one and it is a wonder I can still walk after holding my right foot on the floor at about a 45 degree angle for hours on end. They provide a steady speed, and you can relax a bit and put your legs in more comfortable positions for long drives, like out the window, although the one time I tried that a state trooper pulled up alongside at 65 mph said something unintelligible through this PA system that I assumed was not a compliment on how clean my socks were.

I have put cruise controls in 6 different vehicles and have a perfect installation record, not one has worked on the first test drive. It is helpful to have a degree in mechanical or electrical engineering, or both before you tackle an installation. But usually with a little tinkering and maybe a phone call to the service center in Bombay they will work fine, and using these devices allow me to now walk with only a barely noticeable limp.

Microwave Ovens: From heating up baby bottles to veiled threats aimed towards small pets, microwaves are close to magic. Hot food and drink in a minute or two and if you desire a nice smoky flavor just leave a metal spoon in the dish. Be sure and keep grandpa and his pacemaker at a safe distance while the microwave is in operation though as old folks should not be jumping that high, bad for the hips you know.

Yes microwave ovens are just the nuts for people on the go or people going nowhere but into the living room to sit on their TV dinner butts and enjoy the next essential item.

The VCR. VCR stands for Very Confusing Recorder, which is the conclusion drawn after perusing the owner's manual, but once you've made the flashing 12:00 go away you can record your favorite show even when busy with other things going on in your life, such as putting out the fire in the microwave or making grandpa comfortable on the kitchen floor while awaiting the ambulance.

I guess *TIVO* and other such devices are supposed to be even better and less confusing for recording your TV favorites, but I believe they involve time travel and that freaks me out.

Phone Machines: Yes they are rather impersonal and what you say is recorded of course so watch your words or another word may come back to haunt you. That word would be "evidence." So when you leave a message that at anytime mentions the words "weed" or "grass," you jolly well better be referring to lawn care.

They are also handy for screening calls, and when used in conjunction with Caller ID, you can either not pick up or have some fun with the caller. If it is someone known you answer and say something like; "Hi grandpa, wanna come over and we can microwave up some popcorn, ha, ha, ha...no, I don't suppose it's very funny being in traction..."

WARNING: it is *legal* in 14 states to stalk people who involve young children, pets, stupid humor, or any answering message near or over one minute. A greeting involving kids singing Christmas carols will get you jail time in most Southern states.

A sub-category of useful things is *Remote Controls*. They save a lot of get'n ups and set'n downs. How did our parents ever watch TV without a remote? They had kids. "Turn to channel 4. Turn it up. Turn it down." I was the remote control! It was around the time I turned 12 that my dad finally realized my name wasn't Philco.

I didn't forget computers and cell phones, I just consider them useful tools. If you really need to call or be called a cell phone is invaluable for letting people know what Wal-Mart you are in, and probably the best thing about computers is you can find anything or anyone by using a search engine. So to all the people I've called who had a phone message like this: "Hello, hello, hello...ha, ha, fooled ya. We are not in now so..."

I know where you live.

**The original Miranda Warning:
"Hey, Miranda! Stop or we'll
shoot your sorry ass!"**

Sympathy and glad tidings for the sunburned alcoholic bill paying criminal.

HAL-MARK CARDS

WHEN YOU REALLY DON'T CARE
IF YOU SEND THE VERY BEST

I think I am going to start a greeting card company, seriously. They can't cost that much to produce and most of those things are pretty expensive to buy when you consider they are nothing more than a folded piece of heavy paper or light cardboard, maybe a little art work, and some sappy, questionable sentiment thought up by a stranger who may or may not have at one time worked for the suicide prevention hotline, or called it.

While at the card rack I spotted a note of sympathy for a deceased pet, and it is not unusual to see the occasional "Congratulations On Your Divorce," card. I am sure there are more of this type of unconventional cards people apparently buy, so it occurred to me there might be a small but possibly lucrative business in producing perhaps even a tad more unusual greeting cards for special occasions not normally covered by any other card company. Here are six examples.

(1) Let's start with a seasonal and topical issue, especially for those who live in colder climes. Outside cover of card: *In deepest and most sincere sympathy for the extraordinary, outrageous, unjust, and oppressively high and likely gouged natural gas and electric prices you have been forced to endure.* Inside of card: We share your pain as you struggle to pay the power companies bill, and pray you find solace in knowing an early spring shall bring you warmth, comfort and relief from the travails of winter. Your money is not gone, not forgotten. No, it will be funneled into the giant oil lobby and huge contributions to politicians, and thus shall, in a small way, live forever in off-shore accounts.

(2) How about some happy thoughts for those who may have experienced a bright spot in their criminal career. Outside of card: *Congratulations on successfully bonding out of the pokey!*

Inside of card: (Good Rap lyrics here, incidentally) We know you "did it," and you know it too, but your lawyer got you sprung, the judge is a fool. So enjoy your freedom as long as it lasts, 'cause soon enough in prison they'll be kick'n your...

(3) Once in awhile pleasant diversions unfortunately go wrong, often times with colorful consequences. *So sorry to hear of your severe and discomforting sunburn.* Time and a good aloe lotion will heal all pain, and be assured; when the

redness is gone you will have some semblance of a tan after all. And to comfort you, always remember, if it were the dead of winter you could be paying extraordinary, outrageous, unjust and oppressively high and likely gouged natural gas and electric bills. May the Lord bless and keep you from peeling.

(4) Sometimes people need affirmation that their efforts and struggles are not going un-noticed. *Way to Go! We just knew you and Mr. Sobriety were going to be the best of friends!* There was no doubt in our mind, you could go all this time, without a bottle, or can, in your hand. Don't blame you for brag'n, how you stayed on that wagon, and can now walk, and talk, and stand! A toast to you, and the drinks are on me!

(5) Recognition for a continued level of success in someone's professional career. *So, you fooled them again! Here's to another profitable term, Senator!*

Who would have thought you could have talked your way into office again! Luckily that little problem with the (check one) call girl, Boy Scout, IRS, illegal substance, pony, never came to trial. Just remember to thank all your loyal voters, the living and the dead (applicable in Chicago,) and to abide by these immortal words. "Ask not what you can do for your constituents; ask what union leaders can do for you." Be sure to keep on sucking up to the giant oil lobby and you can probably stay in office forever!

(6) How about a little note of support when someone is working to overcome a certain type of medical condition. Front of card: *So happy to hear you are making such a stand-up effort against your medical problem!* Inside: We know "Bob Dole" disease is not life threatening, and certainly not a hard thing to live with when compared to other medical problems, but you have always been the type of person who has been able to keep at least a stiff upper lip when all else has failed. We have no doubt there will be some down turns ahead as you limp down the road to

recovery, but with the proper medication and therapy you should be living large in as little as fourteen minutes and for up to 4 hours thereafter. And in times of strife such as these you often pretend to be a hard-case, but we know you are really just an old softy, or so goes the rumors. But don't be blue! Stand firm and we know you will be pointing the way for all of us very soon. Keep it up!

HALMARK: When you care enough, to note the un-noteworthy.

As you grow older it's not so much about the things in life you didn't accomplish, but more of the things you did, minus the felonies of course.

Climb a little higher on the tower!

I received a nice new cell phone for Christmas, replacing the one I got a few years back that replaced the first one bought in 1994, and no it was not a bag phone. The new phone works just great, but the transition between the first and second phone was not so smooth.

The phone from 1994 was pretty big but better than previous versions of cell phone technology, the slightly smaller than the walkie-talkie looking gizmos that themselves were a vast improvement over the bag variety that basically started the whole cell phone phenomena.

I miss bag phones. As they were bulky people tended to stay in their cars more when calling as compared to now and so were less likely to carry on a running cell phone conversation on the merits of one feminine hygiene product over another while waiting in the order line at Taco Bell.

My first phone was big enough to perhaps use as a self defense weapon if needed, and I found if you held it just right it could possibly pass for a hand gun in low light situations, so if confronted by some robber/mugger/rapist/census taker type of person you could maybe bluff your way out of danger by waving it madly about and shouting a lot.

And for everybody that asked, yes it was an old cell phone in my pocket and yes I was happy to see you.

I got the second phone with the same provider and told them I really wanted to step up to modern technology and convenience. I too wanted to be able to fumble for a ringing phone in the darkness of a movie theater, and accidentally drop that little sucker in the toilet at least once a year.

But most importantly I want to be able to call in the accident I just caused by yapping when I should have been driving. Sign me up for that nifty little flip phone there. No, I don't need a camera phone... well yes, that would be handy to have at the accident scene.

I was soon on my way with the new phone, and a more expensive calling plan that included "free" minutes every month that rolled over. While toying with the phone some button was accidentally pushed and the thing started to vibrate. I dropped it on the car floor thinking I was getting an electrical shock, but can now understand and appreciate why this feature would get your full attention while stuck in the pocket of your jeans when a call comes in.

When folded up and tucked into its vinyl case it was no bigger than a medium size muffin and likely of no use what so ever as a weapon of self defense like the other one, because I am pretty sure waving around what could be a muffin of some sort wrapped in vinyl and shouting a lot is not going to scare very many people unless they have an un-natural fear of baked goods wrapped in upholstery.

Out of curiosity I went to the post office and used their mail scale to weigh the phone. That little wonder of technology which can allow a person to speak to virtually any place on the planet came in under 3 ounces. The instruction manual however weighed more than 7. Granted half of the book was in a foreign language, which explains why there are so many people speaking some lingo into a cell phone that a lot us can't understand. Obviously and mistakenly they opened the wrong side of the instruction book and now have to phone-talk the language in which they learned how to use it. Yeah, I'm sure that's it...

This particular dip into the then modern technology was rather short lived however. I thought it would be a good idea to use the cell more and save a few bucks on the land line. Problem is the wonder of communication that would allow me to speak to someone in Zimbabwe, if I knew anyone in Zimbabwe, is virtually worthless in the particular cell area where I live.

Turns out I am in a "dead zone" that is not very well covered by my provider's cell towers. I contacted their main office using my home phone, the one with the big round dial, and told them it was my thought that I could better contact people and have a clearer conversation if I climbed one of their towers and just shouted. The nice lady in customer service said this was not uncommon and a lot of their customers indeed did just that, but there was an additional service charge involved.

I wondered if I could even call the new phone using the land line phone sitting next to me and whine to myself about my cell phone situation. Imagine my surprise when the display on my new cell phone announced that I was unavailable.

My first thought was that I had probably just taken the phone off the hook so I wouldn't have to listen to myself whine, but then reality set in. The whole system was worthless unless I traveled out of my weak cell area to make a call and I did not see any allowances for travel credit or mileage in the contract.

I took the little flip phone back the next day and said it would not work for me. "Yeah, we get that a lot from your area," the girl behind the counter told me in a far away and scratchy voice. Got my money back except for a service charge, even though I told her I'd chickened out half way up the tower.

I found another carrier with a lower monthly fee, and free non flip phone the size of a candy bar but weighed less and had virtually no calories, and although there were less free minutes available per month that was plenty of talk time for me and my needs. And as I am interested in and an expert on geography. I would find it very interesting to have a phone friend in Zimbabwe as it is always nice to get to know people in all of the 57 states.

Being eccentric comes from a combination of being weird and having money. Without the money you are just weird.

Helium in the land of OZ.

"Oh joy, rapture. I've got a brain!" So said the Scarecrow upon receiving his gift from the Wizard of Oz. I had reason to recall this classic movie line while attending a function incorporating a Wizard of Oz theme. They had people dressed as Oz characters, Oz decorations, Oz music, and helium balloons. I like helium balloons.

I can't remember when I first learned to make funny voices with helium or who showed me, but I recall for some reason their voice was very high. All I know is you can always get a laugh from helium balloon abuse, and if someone isn't laughing it might be because they have tiny little Munchkin voices and don't find you amusing. That in itself is amusing and therefore you won't need any helium, just engage them in conversation and try not to giggle or snort whatever you are drinking out your nose as you listen to them talk.

I was at another event where I happened upon this lady telling a joke to a small group of people, while apparently under the influence of a *really big* helium balloon. As she spoke and then engaged in a kind of chattering laugh upon reaching the punch line, she sounded like Alvin the Chipmunk on speed. I thought, wow, what endurance. Just about the time I was praising her on the great Munchkin-like imitation she did while telling the joke, I looked around and noticed there were no helium balloons in the room. If the dirty looks from her were water and I was a Wicked Witch, I would have melted into the floor.

I mention endurance because while at the above referenced Oz event there was a lady who was trying to take a helium breath and say, "follow the yellow brick road," and failing miserably. As the Old Pro I grabbed a balloon to show her how it's done, took a big breath and launched into a dead-on and stunning rendition of, *"we represent the lollypop guild, the lollypop guild, the lollypop guild, and in the name of the lollypop guild... (Held guild extra long here) we'd like to welcome you to Munchkin Land."*

I was rewarded with much laughter and applause while I leaned against a chair as the edges of my peripheral vision went away and I seemed to just get heavier and heavier, which is odd as helium is supposedly lighter than air. Apparently my own personal helium endurance is not what it used to be and rave reviews or not I went past my limit. Then of course it was sit down or fall down time, but by golly they were impressed and entertained and that is what's important when playing the fool for an audience, as any fool worth his fake vomit would tell you.

Even a small audience, but we must learn our limits. Years ago while visiting a couple who ran a floral and balloon shop, I walked in the back door and found myself alone and face to nozzle with a big tank of helium. What an extraordinary opportunity to really give my friends a show and provide them with a big laugh! This had the possibility of being the best helium gag ever, surpassing all other mundane attempts from wedding receptions and funerals past. Possibly even better than belching the alphabet after sucking on a big helium balloon, and let me tell you, you could quite easily hack up a lung doing that if you are not careful. This hit was going to be right from the fountain head so to speak and as such is not for the faint of heart, heavy smokers, or anyone with the commons sense of an acorn.

So I sucked up a big double lung full straight from the tank and while holding my helium infused breath strode confidently towards my friends in the next room. Unfortunately they were standing about thirty feet away and the last ten or so feet were a bit of a foggy blur as I recall and I instantly forgot whatever clever and hilarious thing I was going to say, but I got there, laid my head down on the counter and said in a voice that sounded like Mickey Mouse, "I don't feel so good." They thought it was hilarious. "No, really, I think I'm gonna hurl..." (held *hurl* extra long here) I think they wet themselves. I thought at that moment maybe I should join HAA, (Helium Abusers Anonymous.) To bad I hadn't brought my fake vomit.

You see it is not the helium itself that can make you a bit woozy as helium is a colorless, odorless, non-toxic monatomic gas, in fact deep sea divers use a mixture of oxygen, nitrogen, and helium to help them stave off the effects of nitrogen narcosis, which is high pressure nitrogen having a narcotic effect on the brain...but hell everybody knows that. Hearing deep sea divers talk to each other in their undersea-type units while breathing the helium enriched air is like listening in on a Munchkin family reunion.

Pure helium simply takes the place of oxygen temporarily when you take a big breath and that can't be good for brain cells but if we had any brains we wouldn't be gulping down helium in the first place now would we! I am convinced there are certain areas of the country where helium gas is actually pumped into polling places and other venues. This would of course account for the last three democratic administrations and may have played a part in Taylor Hicks winning American Idol.

Why do we do this to ourselves? What do we have to do to stop? Why do we think it's funny? Why *is* it funny? What would a Munchkin sound like on helium...?

I only made it to one HAA meeting and it didn't go very well. As I stood up and said, "Hi, my name is Hal, and..." took a big hit off a helium balloon at this point, "I can sound just like Tinkerbelle!"

As they dragged me out I noticed the Scarecrow wasn't in attendance. He has a brain.

Don't the words creditor and predator sound frighteningly alike?

Press this if you ever want to see your mower again!

Maybe you just want to place an order by phone for some product, schedule an appointment, check a bank or credit card balance, or just for a fun prank turn in your neighbor for cheating on his taxes. It's not true but until he brings back the lawn mower he borrowed two years ago it would be hilarious to watch him squirm, and by now you have probably noticed there are very few live people answering phones anymore.

There are so many automated messaging systems nowadays that live operators are no longer needed, and these systems are so easy to install and maintain that some companies are actually hiring the deceased to oversee their operation with many of them having previously held key White House staff and political advisory positions, while dead. Here are a few samples of what you might hear.

Uh oh, it's not computing. *"This is the computer repair service. If you want this service in English, press 1. To speak to someone with an unintelligible accent, press 2. To speak to a person who has no idea what they are doing, press 3. If you want someone who speaks English, does not have an unintelligible foreign accent and really does knows what they are doing, please hang up now. That option does not exist. Thank you."*

Even the medical profession is going automated.

"Hello, you have reached the doctor's office, if this is a medical emergency, please go to the emergency room nearest you as we don't want you around here anyway if you are contagious, bleeding or throwing up or stuff like that, it's just gross. In the mean time take a couple aspirins and some prune juice or something, and don't call us we'll call you after we get this pesky medical malpractice suit settled. Thanks."

Got an issue with your driver's license? *"This is the Drivers License Bureau; in an effort to serve your licensing needs better we now have an automated system where practically all licensing procedures can be handled over the phone just as efficiently and quickly as being here in person...what, is that laughing I sense? You better not be laughing! If you are calling about getting a drivers license please be prepared to provide us with the following information: Full name, maiden name if applicable, date of birth, city of birth, time of birth, name of attending doctors and nurses, mother's maiden name, fathers maiden name, all brothers and sisters, aunts, uncles, cousins, and grandparents maiden names and their birth dates, city of birth, etc, etc. We will also need your Social Security number, tax records, proof of US citizenship, proof of insurability, references, passport and birth certificate in triplicate. If you cannot provide this information you will be denied a license but should have no problem running for President. An extensive written exam along with a very complex driving test will be given and you must pass both before a drivers license will be granted, unless of course you are in this country illegally then just stop in, we have one ready for you to pick up. Drive carefully, on the right side of the road by the way, and have a nice day."*

Tax problems? Just call the new user friendly IRS. *"You have reached the Internal Revenue Service. Please be assured that as a government agency we have your best interest at heart and are here to help you...laughing, do I sense laughing? Please use your touch tone phone to input your Social Security number, and please do not worry that this will somehow get into the wrong hands as it most certainly already has. More people have seen your Social Security number than the Halloween fright mask Nancy Pelosi constantly wears. Please enter your SS number now, and if you can't remember the number don't worry we can easily obtain it from some 10 year old hacker or your computer technician with the unintelligible foreign accent. Please provide us with a current phone number, we guarantee this will not be sold or rented to any telemarketer. They all have it on file anyway; in fact we buy phone numbers from them. We have made every effort to make your tax paying simpler, so please follow these two easy steps. STEP 1: Key in or speak clearly into the phone your total income from last year. STEP 2: Send it in. All of it, we are serious. Thank you. I don't hear you laughing now, and by the way your neighbor really was cheating on his taxes, thanks. Sorry, we had to sell your mower."*

Got bad cable TV reception? *"Hello, you have reached the automated help line for your TV cable service. Please press 1 if you have a blank screen. Press 2 if the image is fuzzy. Press 3 if all you can get on your TV is Jerry Springer. Press 4 if that makes you so (bleep'n) mad you want to personally slap that miserable (bleep) right off the (bleep'n) stage. Please hold for our technical department, but first please be sure your TV and cable box are both plugged into an operational electrical outlet. We know this is basic common sense, but if you had any basic common sense you would have switched to satellite by now. We want to remind you that prompt payment of your TV cable charge is both important and appreciated. By the way your bill is going up 25% next month and we are removing 6 more channels."*

"You have reached the Congressional switchboard. Nobody here has a freaking clue what we are doing, but we are going to keep on spending your tax money like drunken monkeys on speed anyway. (Bleep) you very much."

There is just not enough time in a day for all the inefficiency I have to accomplish.

The truth about fiberglass.

I was doing some repair work on the fiberglass nose of my Formula Vee race car some time back, the nose often being the first thing to arrive at the scene of an accident, and as fiberglass repair kits are readily available for general fix-it projects and with me being pretty well versed in this material I was inspired to share my hard earned knowledge with you in the event you ever need to do some "glassing." Just sign this release form.

My first experience was fixing a hole in a fiberglass garage door, and although not very neat or attractive it was quite functional and managed to keep out most of the larger animals. Unfortunately I had not fully honed my glassing repair skills when I sold the fiberglass boat with a "patched" hole in it to the lawyer from Missouri. I know that sounds mighty risky, but somehow just seemed so satisfyingly right.

The components of fiberglass are resin and hardener. Resin is the honey looking thick liquid that comes in a can and the hardener which is in a small tube. You mix the two together and a chemical reaction will occur causing heat and "curing." When used in conjunction with fiberglass mat or cloth it becomes very strong when applied to most everything except maybe boats owned by southern lawyers. The mat type material is rougher and thicker and often times used to build up an area. The cloth is the silkier looking material that is mainly utilized for finish work on your project.

You "wet" the mat or cloth piece with the mix using a throw away foam brush and stick it where it belongs. Caution: Where ever you stick it is going to stay stuck for a long time, with the possible exception being the above mentioned boat that may or may not be currently resting on the bottom of some lake in the Ozarks.

As a disclaimer I have to mention that much of my experience and knowledge had its beginnings with an unfortunate incident a long time ago while working on an airplane project where I inadvertently fiberglassed a hat to my head. Got the form sighed? Let us begin.

Fiberglass does not come gently out of ones hair. (See above).

Fiberglass comes from the Greek words "Fiberis" which translates to "makes you," and Glassis" that means "itch all over."

To speed up the curing process it is beneficial to add 2-3 times the normal amount of hardener to the resin, but you must work with haste.

2-3 times the normal amount of hardener added to the resin in a plastic cup will melt the bottom out of said cup if you are a bit on the slow side with that haste thing.

An inadvertent bug or two...or 20, in your resin/hardener mix will make good filler, as does hair. (See above).

It is best to work the wet fiberglass while wearing disposable rubber or plastic gloves. Always, always remove the wet gloves before scratching your head. (See above). If using the bare handed method of laying wet fiberglass, a good way to clean up your hands afterward is to use a rag or paper towel dampened with an amount of Acetone. This will clean up your sticky hands quite quickly not to mention how well it will alert you to even the tiniest abrasions in your skin. Acetone also melts most plastics. Do not carelessly toss the damp acetone rag on your cordless phone handset lying there on your work bench.

A little bit of tobacco or ash from a cigar in your fiberglass mix will hurt nothing. A little fiberglass mix on a cigar will greatly alter the taste and make it burn really, really fast.

Grinding and sanding fiberglass is very dusty work. A cheap dust mask and goggles is better than nothing at all, and if you wear a large garbage bag over your clothes it will help keep some of the dust off, but may frighten your dog and puzzle the neighbors.

One beer makes the dusty fiberglass taste in your mouth go away. Six beers make the rationale for workings with fiberglass go away.

If you wear the same clothes every time you work with fiberglass and wipe your sticky hands on your trousers often, it is entirely possible you will have a pair of pants that will be able to stand in the corner on their own. However, they make excellent exhaust vent ducting for your clothes dryer.

Scratching ones behind with sticky fiberglassy fingers then sitting down on the lady of the houses best sofa, will unleash the Dogs of Hell.

If you get a little fiberglass mix in your eye, rinse with clean water and immediately seek medical care. If you get a substantial amount of fiberglass mix in your eye, get used to the nickname "Patch."

Although it is very pretty, do not try and make fiberglass cloth into undergarments.

It is always better to have a fat check book and get someone else to do your fiberglass work than to do it yourself.

I hope this has been helpful. Thank you. Oh, and please only mention my name in hushed tones while in Missouri.

Cherish, is the word.

The Association, 1966

The last chase.

It doesn't seem that long ago grandpa, you pulled the old bi-plane out of the barn where it wintered. We washed and cleaned that magnificent bird until it looked like new again.

"Now Grandpa, now?" I asked, my little 12 year old body shaking with anticipation. "Not now," you said. I knew you enjoyed working on the plane, and making me wait!

We ate sandwiches grandma brought us while sitting in the shade of the wing and watching the high clouds pass by so slowly it was like trying to see the minute hand move on your gold pocket watch. "Looks like it's almost ready" I said. "Yes it does" you replied. "Now?" I said, trying to act nonchalant. You weren't buying the cool act. "Maybe later."

You filled the gas tank and I polished and buffed the propeller spinner, then suddenly, we were finished.

I looked up at the tall weathered man whose hair seemed almost as white as the clouds above him. You knew the look. "Soon, I'm sure it will be very soon."

We stood for several minutes and watched the shiny blue plane moving ever so slightly in the light breeze. Then there it was. We both saw it at the same time.

"That's the one!" you said. Your voice held the excitement that I felt. "Get in, you know what to do." I hopped into the front cockpit and opened the throttle just a notch with one hand and flipped the switch with the other, you already had both hands on the propeller. "Contact?" you yelled. "Contact!" I yelled back. With a downward pull you flipped the prop and puffs of blue-white smoke belched from the exhaust, with a pop, then another, now a rumble, now a roar! First try!

You were never so spry as when you climbed into that rear cockpit for the first flight of spring. Picking up speed on the grass runway we pulled down our goggles, and as the plane went faster and faster we soon had that happy feeling as the bouncing and shaking stopped. We were flying!

As we climbed all before us was blue sky and tall clouds through the whirling propeller. Turning gently we both saw our quest, a low cloud all by itself and moving fast, but it was our cloud and we had to catch it!

We flew as fast as the old plane would take us. Indeed we were flying faster than the clouds themselves, faster than any bird, faster than anyone had ever flown before...or it seemed so. We could not let this cloud, our cloud, get away. We hadn't missed one since you first strapped me into the plane when I was so small I had to sit on four extra cushions just to see out of the cockpit.

We flew faster and more determined than ever before. I could feel the intensity coming from the back cockpit. Somehow this was different than the other times. Special.

Closer...closer... Our cloud grew bigger and bigger. We must be almost upon it!

Mist. Vapor. The blue sky above us went away. The earth below all but disappeared. The roar of the motor and wind lowered as you pulled back the throttle. We caught it. Your eyes were bright with a happy and peaceful smile. Slowly we raised our hands into the rushing air, and then as we had done so many times before on the first flight of the year, we moved our hands in the shape of letters. We wrote our names on that cloud. This was our cloud, our sky, our airplane. Our moment.

We savored the victory for a little while, then dived out of the cloud back to where the sky is blue and earth is green. Spring and summer now had their proper beginning.

That headlong dash across the sky to sign a cloud was to be our last. It *was* special and ever so cherished. In the years since, I get out his pocket watch and smile as I look at the minute hand and remember the high clouds we watched go slowly by in the spring, and the low fast ones we caught and owned...if just for a moment.

But oh, what a moment!

Links

Autobahn Country Club: www.autobahncc.com

Blackhawk Farms Raceway: www.blackhawkfarms.com

Bureau County Republican: www.bcrnews.com

Greg Wallace, Blog: www.gregwallace.wordpress.com

Hal Adkins, Blog: www.haladkinsaintnormal.com

La Moille, IL: www.buffalodays.org

Lulu.com: www.lulu.com

Midwestern Council of Sports Car Clubs:
www.mcscc.org

Road America: www.roadamerica.com

Sports Car Club of America: www.scca.com

Sports Car Club of America, Chicago Region:
www.scca-chicago.com

Sports Car Club of America, Milwaukee Region:
www.scca-milwaukee.org

State of Florida: www.visitflorida.com

Vintage Sports Car Drivers Association: www.vscda.org

Wounded Warrior Project:
www.woundedwarriorproject.org

WZPH Oldies Radio: www.rdray.com/WZPH

The bleep'n end!